The Long, Steep Path

Everyday inspiration from the author of
Pay It Forward

CATHERINE
RYAN HYDE

THE LONG, STEEP PATH: EVERYDAY INSPIRATION
FROM THE AUTHOR OF *PAY IT FORWARD*.

Copyright © 2013 by Catherine Ryan Hyde.

We can find the life we want.
It's hiding in plain sight ... in the life we have now.

If you believe that life is a journey, that we can't hold still even if we tried, then THE LONG, STEEP PATH: EVERYDAY INSPIRATION FROM THE AUTHOR OF *PAY IT FORWARD* is the gentle, thoughtful, and wholly entertaining roadmap to a happy life of self-knowledge and creative inspiration, from someone who has been through it all.

"What inspired you to write the novel Pay It Forward?"

Years after the publication of *Pay It Forward*, this is still the most common question asked of Catherine Ryan Hyde, bestselling and critically acclaimed author of more than 18 novels for adults and young adults, including *Pay It Forward,* the incredible bestselling novel that led to a movie, a foundation, and an entire social movement.

Everything *Pay It Forward* became, it turns out, is rooted in a small, but extraordinary act of kindness, which Catherine received as a young adult. It was one life moment that caused her to look at life in a different way, changing all other life moments that followed. It was a moment of true inspiration.

A few years before she began to pursue her dream of being a writer, Catherine's life was spiraling into depression and addiction. And now … it's not. And it hasn't been for nearly a quarter of a century. Changing your life isn't easy, but Catherine started with the most ordinary ingredients. She started with the life she had. And she found her inspiration.

In THE LONG, STEEP PATH: EVERYDAY INSPIRATION FROM THE AUTHOR OF *PAY IT FORWARD*, Catherine shares her journey, as well as what inspires her, in a series of funny and totally engaging stories that manage to be at once intimate and universal. This is the rare inspirational book that even the most cynical reader can love.

The Long, Steep Path

Introduction

By a huge margin, this is the most common question I receive:

"What was your inspiration for the novel *Pay It Forward*?"

This is always my answer:

It was 1978, my memory tells me. If it wasn't, it was close enough to 1978 to pass. I was driving my car, an aging, miserably maintained Datsun (translation for younger people: Nissan) in a bad Los Angeles neighborhood late at night.

I was alone.

Not such a great idea, I know, but I lived in that bad neighborhood, which narrowed my options considerably. Let's face it. We all have to go home.

That my car was in such miserable condition was nobody's fault but my own. I was young in 1978. I was in my early twenties, and I had this theory: it was cheaper to just drive your car and *not* take it to the mechanic. People laugh when I say that, but it made perfect sense to me at the time. Mechanics cost money, right? Therefore, if you don't go to them, you save money. *Right?* It's thinking reserved for the new driver, and one of those theories that works fairly well until the day it doesn't anymore.

This was that day.

I reached the stop sign at the end of the freeway ramp at Echo Park Lake. I put my foot on the brake, and the engine stalled. This might sound unusual to you, but the engine always stalled when I took my foot off the gas. It's what happens when you never take your car to the mechanic. You feed it gas, or it doesn't run. It's the price you pay for youthful theories.

I reached for the ignition to start it up again, and all the electricity on my car suddenly died. Headlight, dash lights . . . out. Now I was in a bad neighborhood late at night *in the dark*.

At this juncture I was indeed surprised. The car had never done this before. If it had, I would have found the money somewhere. That's one of the flaws in my theory. The money you say you don't have appears out of nowhere when the car behaves *this* badly. But of course by then it was too late.

I noticed a curl of smoke.

I almost don't need to go any further for you to know that this is the bad news part of the story. Smoke is never good news in any driving story, and this story is no exception. The smoke was curling up from underneath the dashboard, on the driver's side. It didn't take a high school graduate (or an expensive mechanic) to figure out that it was coming through the firewall from the engine compartment, and that it would soon fill up the passenger area where I needed to sit.

Whether you've tried it for yourself or not (and please don't) you probably know that when you're in a bad neighborhood late at night, you feel a powerful incentive to stay in your car with the doors locked. Until the car fills up with smoke. This might very well be the textbook definition of being "between a rock and a hard place."

I jumped out. Into the bad neighborhood. Alone.

Or so I thought.

I looked up to see two men, two total strangers, running in my direction Very fast. One of them was carrying a blanket.

Many thoughts danced in my head. I think the first was, *I never made out a will.* Then I realized it didn't matter, because I had nothing to leave to anybody, anyway. Except the car. Which was on fire.

Probably other thoughts danced around in there as well. But I can tell you one thought I'm sure did not dance: *rescue.* The crazy idea that these men might be coming to my rescue was, unfortunately, nowhere on the list. Not even *far down* on the list. I could claim it was all the way at the bottom, or on the reverse side, but I'd be lying. Rescue missed the list entirely.

And yet, as it turned out, they were coming to my rescue.

One of the men pushed past me and popped the hood of my car from the inside. The other, the man with the blanket, opened the hood, leaned his entire upper body into my flaming engine compartment, and put the fire out using only the blanket and his bare hands.

I just want to pause here, briefly, for emphasis. *His* bare hands. *My* flaming engine compartment. Isn't that a fascinating combination between total strangers? I thought so, too.

Right around the time they put out the fire, the fire department showed up. And I have no idea who called them. When speaking to groups of kids, as I often have, they like to posit that someone had a cell phone and I didn't notice. No. Not in 1978. No one had a cell phone. This was back when we had emergency call boxes on the highway. (I guess we still do, but we ignore them, because we all have cell phones.) Apparently someone going by on the freeway behind us had seen the trouble I was in and stopped to call the fire department.

Now, I certainly would call the fire department for a stranger. I hope most of us would. For anyone. But would I lean my upper body into a stranger's flaming engine compartment and put out the fire with my bare hands?

This, of course, is the sixty-four-dollar question ... even today. I know that, at the time, the answer would have been *no*.

By the time the fire department arrived, there wasn't much left for them to do. The fire was already out. They came roaring up with the lights flashing and the siren screaming, and ... well ... frankly, it was anticlimactic. So they just helped us push my Datsun over to the side of the road. They showed me how the fire had started. (Not interesting). And they explained what would have happened if it hadn't been put out. (Not happy, but interesting.)

Though we don't like to think in these terms as we drive, and I'm not suggesting you do, a car is put together much like a Molotov cocktail. It's a container of flammable liquid, with a fuse (fuel line) running into it. The only real difference is that you don't pick up the car and throw it. But a firebomb is a firebomb.

That's when I realized: these two men had saved more than just my car. They may have saved my life, or saved me from injuries I prefer not to contemplate. And in the process they may have put their own lives at risk.

I turned around to thank them, and discovered that they had already packed up and driven away. In the confusion of talking to the fire department, they'd left. And I hadn't noticed. And I hadn't even said thank you. This had been the biggest favor I'd ever received, and from total strangers. And I could not rely on the certainty of seeing them again, because LA's not a that small a town.

So what do you do with a favor that big if you can't pay it back?

I've had many people ask me, in response to that story, "So, you're saying that if they hadn't stopped that night, the whole *Pay It Forward* thing never would have happened?" And I say, "I'll take it a step further than that. If they hadn't left without saying goodbye, there never would have been a *Pay It Forward* novel." And, if there hadn't been the novel, there wouldn't have been the movie, the foundation, the movement. If those two strangers had stayed around to absorb my gratitude, I simply might have gotten their names and sent them a Christmas card every year for the rest of our natural lives. And that might have felt like enough.

But they left.

Amazingly, I was able to get the car fixed. And then I went back to driving the freeways for my business. But something had changed.

Me.

Suddenly I had one eye on the side of the road, looking for someone broken down, or otherwise in trouble. And I knew that when I saw such a person, I would stop. And of course I did stop. Even though I never had before.

And here comes the answer to the sixty-four-dollar question: I now drive with a fire extinguisher in my trunk. Because, you know, given my unusual personal history on the subject, I'd feel far too guilty if I ignored a car-fire victim and kept driving. It's just not the way life is supposed to go. But I still don't like the bare-hands/fire equation. This way, I figure I can toss them the fire extinguisher and call out, "Pay It Forward!" before going on my merry way and purchasing a re-placement. That works. Right?

Anyway, my point is … that act of kindness changed me.

And, because it did, I began watching to see if other acts of kindness changed other people as well. And, almost invariably, I saw that they did. I observed small acts of kindness changing people in smalls ways. And I felt I'd already proved that a big enough act of kind-ness can alter the course of a person's life entirely. But, big or small, I've still yet to see the recipient remain unchanged.

Years later I got serious about becoming a writer, and a year or two after that *Pay It Forward* got serious about becoming a book.

And that is one example of the inspiration I've found in my life through a single incident. It's one life moment that caused me to look at my life in a different way, changing all the other life moments that followed.

Of course, there have been—and will continue to be—many others, most less smoky and dramatic, and generally much smaller in scope. But they all have one thing in common: the sense of life subtly shifting the direction of my travel through the world. And I do firmly believe that this life is a journey. Hard though we may try, we can't successfully hold still. It seems to be a process of moving along, one step at a time, to achieve a goal—such as a summit—only to learn there are other peaks and valleys beyond. (I think my penchant for steep hiking factors into this metaphor. But more about that later on.)

The trouble with inspiration, even for an old veteran author like myself, is that it's often hard to shrink a concept so huge into the confines of words. Stories can easily illustrate it, yet I'm not convinced that words can contain it.

But, difficult though inspiration may be to pin down, I find it fairly easy to recognize. So I've arranged my thinking on the premise that it's a bit like old Supreme Court definition of pornography: I can't define it, exactly, but I know it when I see it

I can easily report words that have inspired me, but I can't really say why they did. Someone else might have said the same thing to me earlier to no effect, or the same words might have meant little if said to someone else, or by someone else.

I can (and do!) report how often I find inspiration in nature, but I can't fully explain what it is I find there. I bask in it, but I can't break it down into its elements. The elusive missing link strikes me as nothing less than the proverbial "ghost in the machine," as impossible to define as the spirit that animates a living being.

At the end of the prologue in my novel *Pay It Forward*, the reporter character, Chris Chandler, says a couple of sentences that seem to be quoted more often than any other lines from the book. He says, "Knowing it started from unremarkable circumstances should be a comfort to us all. Because it shows you don't need much to change the entire world for the better. You can start with the most ordinary ingredients. You can start with the world you've got."

So, it seems to me, it is with an individual life. We can find the life we want. It's hiding in plain sight. Where? Where else … in the life we have now.

I say this with some confidence, as I've done it myself. Just a few years before I began to pursue my dream of being a writer, my life was going around in a circle. In fact, if I were to be quite honest, it was circling the proverbial bowl, spiraling down into alcohol and drug addiction, and depression.

And now it's … not. And it hasn't been for nearly a quarter of a century.

As best I can figure as of this writing, I made these changes by asking more of myself. But not by asking *too much* of myself.

By letting the people around me inspire and direct and help and change me. But still spending time in solitude.

By staying in the moment as much as possible.

And accepting what is.

By letting life itself inspire and direct and help and change me.

And, possibly most importantly, by being grateful for the good things I already have.

It's not often easy, but it may be simpler than it seems. We can start with the most ordinary ingredients. We can start with the life we've got.

Ask More of Yourself

The Grand Canyon

The Award Venue

For more photos related to this story:
http://www.catherineryanhyde.com/the-long-steep-
path/grand-canyon/

The first time I ever set my sights on a big hike, it was a day hike of the Grand Canyon. That's not to say it was the first hike I ever did. On the contrary, to go straight from being a nonhiker to trekking from the south rim to the Colorado River and back, all in one day … well, that would be … not a good idea. I was tempted to say "suicidal," but there's some chance you might not literally die. There is no chance, however, that you wouldn't *wish* you were dead.

What I did was *set my sights* on this hike. Because I love the Grand Canyon so much. Because every time I'd been there I'd watched hikers come up from below the rim, and envied them. If only I were in shape to do that! But I was in my late forties. And I had never hiked at that level.

So I couldn't do it.

Right?

Once I began to question that basic assumption, everything changed.

I made reservations at the El Tovar Hotel (this was years before I owned a little motor home) seven months in advance, and planned the hike. Studied the weather, the equipment I would need. Watched videos about the rigors and the pitfalls.

I had seven months to get in shape.

I started with little hills in my area that gained 300 to 500 feet of elevation. And I just kept working up.

A few weeks before the big event, I drove to Pinnacles National Monument and hiked over the tall pinnacles, across the park, then up to Chalone Peak, then back across the pinnacles to my car, for a grand total of sixteen horizontal miles and a mile of vertical gain.

If I could do that, I could do the Grand Canyon.

And I did do the Grand Canyon. And I've done the Grand Canyon two more times since, though the last time I stayed one night at the bottom (at Phantom Ranch), and didn't try to do it all in one day. I day-hiked it twice before. I know I can. But I also know it hurts. A lot.

But back to the first time.

As I hiked, I found myself briefly reflecting on all the hiking I'd done to get ready for this life-changing event.

There was Valencia Peak, about half an hour from my home, with 1,300 feet of vertical gain. I'd done that a dozen times. And its neighbor, Oats Peak, at about the same height. Another dozen there. Nearly twenty trips up Cerro Alto, with a gain of 1,650 feet. Those were my staples, the ones I did most regularly. Then there were a handful of 3,000-foot treks, the Pinnacles test, the Canyon itself ...

I realized that my collective elevation gain was well over 60,000 feet. And that 60,000 feet is higher than the distance a person would have to climb to go from sea level to the top of Mount Everest. Twice.

Now, if you had asked me if I was capable of climbing *the equivalent* (I stress this, because Mount Everest has many special dangers and challenges beyond its elevation gain alone) of the distance from sea level to the top of Mount Everest twice, I'd have laughed at you. I'd have said, "Of course not. No one can. Least of all me."

But I did exactly that, and more.

It just took me seven months.

Once upon a time, when I looked to accomplish something, I tended to want to jump straight to my goal. That's just part of being human, it seems. And when I couldn't get there immediately, I assumed I couldn't get there.

Or, anyway, I said I couldn't.

But maybe what I really meant was that I didn't want it *that* badly. And maybe also that I didn't want it to take that long. I didn't want to have to trudge up fifty different mountains over the course of seven months. I wanted it only if I could just reach out and take it.

Precious few things worth having were ever so immediately within my reach. But, that day in the Grand Canyon, I figured out that almost everything could be accomplished if I wanted it badly enough, and there was no time limit.

This idea opened a door to my seeing that the rigors and trials of a task that big are not brick walls designed to keep me out. They're just pop quizzes to determine how badly I want in.

I had answered the question of whether I was willing to be someone who was brave enough to just keep walking—one of those pathologically stubborn folks who set big goals.

It turned out to be an important question, as I was noticing that life lays aside special rewards for these stubborn ones.

When I finally reached my goal, I found the award venue was not overly crowded. Because most people had already given up and gone home.

This is not unlike the business in which I've chosen to make my living.

Like most writers, I wrote a novel … and expected to publish it. And it seemed I couldn't get there from where I began. But the stories I published in small literary magazines—periodicals with circulations of less than a thousand, of which I can almost guarantee you've never heard—served as stepping stones.

I moved from one to another, creating each stone in front of me before taking another step. And when I got to the goal of publishing a novel, most everybody else had given up and gone home.

It's crowded on the Grand Canyon trails just below the rim. But by the river, eight difficult miles from the hotels and restaurants, I could definitely hear myself think. It's one of the most impressive spots on earth, and, like everything else worth attaining, it's reserved for those who just keep walking.

The Inca Trail to Machu Picchu

Don't Look Up

For more photos related to this story:
http://www.catherineryanhyde.com/the-long-steep-
path/inca-trail-to-machu-picchu/

This segment of my life travel started with an oddly convergent moment.

I was in my bedroom, reading a hiker's magazine with a feature about backpacking the Inca Trail to Machu Picchu. It's a bit of a complicated trip, because it's something that can only be done with an established guide and porters. This is an actual Peruvian regulation. But this article brought it all together and made it feel possible. It even gave details on who to contact, and how to make your plans.

Machu Picchu had long been a dream of mine. And I knew it was a dream my mom had always had. What I didn't know is that you could backpack to the destination.

Well, *I* could. But my mom was eighty-three that year ... I figured Machu Picchu might be a little rich for her blood.

This was the clincher: at the end of the article I found a tip, for those less physically inclined. There's a train. A train transports travelers from Cusco, Peru, to Aguas Calientes, the tiny town at the foot of Machu Picchu. Every day.

I excitedly carried the magazine to the living room to discuss what I'd learned with my mom, who shares my home in her retirement. I wanted to explore the possibility that we could fly to Peru, and she could take the train while I backpacked the trail. When I got to the living room, guess what she was reading? A book that mentioned Machu Picchu, and had started her dreaming again.

It just had that meant-to-be feel.

And so it was.

• • •

My team and I camped the first night at about 13,000 feet, just underneath Dead Woman's Pass.

To look up at it, you wouldn't think it's a particularly vicious piece of trail. The distance and elevation gain of this short segment were about the same as the small training hikes I bite off every four or five days in preparation for a big trip. But you just know there's a catch, don't you? Here's the catch: there's no oxygen up there. Well. Some. But not much.

I woke in the night, and walked a perfectly flat path toward the oddly designed outhouses. Ten steps later I was out of breath. And in the morning, I was supposed to hike up the mountain that loomed above me.

There's a trick to getting lowlanders up these 14,000-foot Peruvian passes. Coca leaves. They can be chewed or made into a tea. I'm sure they speed one up in general, and I've heard they help with the metabolizing of oxygen.

This is all second-hand information. I never chewed coca leaves. I never drank coca tea. As I've already mentioned, I'm a recovering addict and alcoholic. At the time I had about sixteen years clean and sober. I could not picture myself going home to my local twelve-step group and telling them I'd used coca to propel myself over a mountain pass. So I told my guide in advance that I would not be availing myself of the coca method.

Yet in the morning a porter came to my tent, when it was clear I was awake, and brought me a wash basin full of warm water, a washrag, a mug of hot water, and a tray with teas and Nescafé powdered coffee. The tea selection included coca leaves. And I was the only one in the hiking party not on staff. I'll never know whether that's simply how the tray was arranged or whether he was giving me a chance to quietly change my mind now that I knew what I was up against.

I drank Nescafé.

We set off. I walked ten steps uphill and had to stop to breathe. And I don't just mean two or three breaths to catch up. Every ten or twenty steps I got so completely winded that I had to stop and catch my breath again.

This would be a slow ascent.

Then again, where is it written that it must be a fast ascent? Who was timing my ascent?

That's actually a question with an easy answer: *I* was. *I* was the one telling myself I wasn't going fast enough. *I* was the one questioning whether or not I could do it. *I* was the one who kept looking up to the summit to confirm, once again, that it was an unimaginable distance (and elevation gain) away.

Whose side was I on if not my own?

So I stumbled on this piece of advice to give to myself.

"Don't look up."

You thought it was just the opposite, didn't you? You thought the advice was, "Don't look down." It depends, in my opinion. If I were ever on a tightrope (parenthetically, not bloody well likely) I would avoid looking down, knowing it would only alarm me, remind me how much is at stake, and make me that much more likely to fall. But on the Inca Trail to Machu Picchu, trudging to the crest of a pass that rises more than 14,000 feet above sea level, I tried to avoid looking up, because I quickly learned that it would only discourage me and invite my subconscious to question whether I was up to the task.

Which I ... was. But not by such a huge margin that it would have been wise to invite myself to question my abilities.

And, by the way, I get that you're probably not planning to fly to Peru and march up the Inca Trail to the aptly named Dead Woman's Pass. So here's why I'm sharing all this. Because I've found that this same method applies to any type of climbing, real or figurative. If I'm working to ascend anything—a steep piece of trail, my own personal or spiritual growth, or an ambitious goal—I've learned not to keep looking up. It would only remind me what a daunting task I have in front of me. It would only help me be daunted.

I found a way that works much better for me.

Here's what I learned to do, and it helped. A lot.

I focused on the step I was taking. The current one. The now step. I did that over and over. And over. And over. And over. Until I'd taken many more steps than I thought I had in me.

Then I turned around and looked back down the trail.

Wow, I thought. *Wow! I've come a long way. I've climbed high already. Look at those tiny tents down there at camp. Look how high above them I am. I've done a tough segment of this trail. And if I can do the part behind me, I can do the part in front of me.*

In time I crested the pass, my guide took photos, and we—heartbreakingly—descended thousands of feet into a valley. Then we had to gain all that elevation all over again.

This was the toughest day of my three-day, two-night backpack. By far. We couldn't stop and cook lunch until we got to the next pass (it's all very structured on the Inca Trail), which amounted to about 2:30 P.M. By then I was sure this was one of the worst ideas I'd ever had. But after lunch I enjoyed a second wind. The trail leveled just slightly.

The cook from our party passed me on the trail. He said, "You are walking fast, Madame."

I laughed and said, "No, not really. It just seems as if I am. Because I was walking so slowly before."

Camp was not made when I arrived, because I wasn't expected so soon (because I'd been struggling so badly for so long). Did I mind? I did not. I sat on a rock and watched the full moon rise. And I knew in my heart that this was one of the best ideas I'd ever had.

The following morning the sun gleamed off the glacier, and we descended to Machu Picchu. A few hours later I was standing at the Sun Gate, looking down on my dream destination. Knowing my mom was down there waiting to meet up with me again.

Knowing it had all been worth it.

But in the toughest parts of the climb, I didn't know that. So it was essential that I learned to be on my own side, to encourage myself. Only I can control the messages in my head. I may not have installed them, but, with great effort and a lot of practice, I can at least choose what to play at what time.

These are the best two life lessons I ever learned on a tough trail in the great outdoors:

One, not to look up and see how far I still have to climb. Instead to look back and see how far I've climbed already. When I see what I just did, I know I can do what comes next. Given time.

And, two, to give myself time.

Ragged Point

How To Walk Twenty-One Miles

For more photos related to this story:
http://www.catherineryanhyde.com/the-long-steep-
path/ragged-point/

Today, for the fourth or fifth time, I got to do what I consider to be the world's best hike.

Admittedly, this is a highly subjective rating.

Granted, the Big Sur coastline is world-class scenic. But I'm giving this hike big points for ease of getting to the trailhead, and comfort of accommodations at the trailhead.

You see, the trailhead is my front door.

Every once a year or so I like to walk out my front door about fifteen minutes before civil twilight (about an hour before dawn) and keep hiking until I get all the way up the coast to the Ragged Point Inn. It's about twenty and a half to twenty-two miles, depending on whether I follow the shoreline out to the points.

Today's hike was about twenty-one miles.

People ask me all the time how I hike twenty-one miles in one day.

I have several answers. In fact, I have three.

First answer. Short and simple:

I walk down the hill to the ocean, make a right, and keep putting one foot in front of the other until I see the Ragged Point sign.

Second answer. Quite a bit more detailed:

I pack two lunches. Fill a three-liter water bladder with homemade sports drink. Put a few essentials in a daypack. Put on sunscreen, Cool-max sock liners, smart-wool extra-heavy hiking socks, my boots, and a highway safety vest. I also have a bike flag that can stick up a good four feet over my pack. Because a big part of this hike has to be done on the highway shoulder.

If hiking on a highway shoulder sounds anything less than quaint and scenic, rather than continue picturing whatever highway you're picturing, picture Highway One instead. Two lanes, one going north, one going south. Bucolic pastures giving way to green hills on the right. The ocean breathing off to the left against a rocky shore. Not much shoulder. A lot of bends. And a lighthouse off in the distance.

There. That's more like it.

I walk out my front door and down Moonstone Beach Drive by headlamp. By the time I run out of Drive, and have to get on the highway for a stretch, it's civil twilight.

Going through Hearst Ranch country, I pass the Hearst Castle sitting up on the hill, looking unlike anything else in the world. I also pass a lot of cows, horses, bulls butting at flies ... and ... sometimes zebra. Hard to imagine, I know. But they're leftovers from the original Hearst zoo.

Today, sorry. No zebra.

I pass some seals. Not elephant seals, though this hike features many of them as well. Smaller harbor seals. They sun on the rocks. They lift their heads and tails like sideways commas if a wave comes high enough to splash. They shoot me a look as I pass.

And then I pass the even more interesting elephant seals. The bulls have something like a short trunk.

(Does that make it a truncated trunk? Sorry. Never mind.) And they make a noise I could never in a million years describe. That trunk is like an echo chamber. If you want to see it close up, use binoculars or a camera with a strong zoom. Don't go closer. They are wild and more than a little territorial. Oh, and did I mention that they weigh in at around two tons or more? Right. Enough said.

When I get to the lighthouse, I'm about two-thirds of the way there. That's the good news.

Unfortunately, that leaves about seven miles left to go.

San Carpoforo Creek curving and spilling out into the ocean, the site of the actual land feature of Ragged Point, is always a welcome discovery, because it means I only have a mile left to hike.

That's the good news.

Now for the bad news: it's the hardest mile in the history of miles.

It goes sharply uphill, which, after twenty miles of hiking you tend to feel. It has no shoulder to speak of. Very little margin for error. Just the road, barely enough room for a pair of feet, then a guardrail, and a several-hundred-foot drop-off into the sea.

This is where the flag and the vest come in handy. This is where I say a little prayer that the drivers are paying attention.

And then there's the most beautiful sign ever, that Ragged Point sign, and the first snip of blue sky I've seen all day. The fog breaks up just the tiniest bit over the green, green mountains. Enough blue sky to make a coat, as they used to say.

The Ragged Point Inn is a nice place to sit and wait for my ride. And my friend Nancy (my aforementioned ride) brings my Ugg boots, because the hiking boots have got to go after twenty-one miles. And she brings me a blanket to wrap up in (it's surprisingly chilly).

But, for those of you who still don't get how I walk twenty-one miles, here's answer number three:

I don't ever tell myself I can't go that far. And I just don't stop walking.

Hitting Bottom

It's All Clean and Sober From Here

I struck off on my own early in life. Started down my own path, alone, far too sure I could handle things. I "accelerated" through high school, completing four years' worth of study in three years. So I could get out of town. Shortly after I turned seventeen, I moved to New York City. Alone.

The drinking age was eighteen. I was not. But I was close.

It didn't hold me back much.

At the time, some bar and liquor store owners really wanted you to be old enough to drink. Many more only cared that you were old enough to afford to.

It's really remarkable that I survived, since I had a habit of stumbling home with my work girlfriends, leaning on each other and laughing, through the Bronx at about 2:00 A.M.

But somehow I lived long enough to move to California.

Where recreational drugs were ridiculously easy to find.

In retrospect, I guess this allowed me to ice the emotional pain that was nearly as old as I was. Trouble is, I could always still feel it. Just not as acutely. Just not enough to be forced to deal with it. To be forced into any genuine change.

I blinked a couple of times, watched the earth spin faster with each passing year. And then I was nearly thirty-four.

I wasn't living under a bridge. I hadn't gotten a DUI. I had never been arrested. So, that's good, right? Now for the down side. I hadn't done much of *anything*.

I hadn't held a job for long. I never got fired, but my messy life grew too visible when I stayed in one place, so I kept moving.

I hadn't had much success with relationships. And it's probably just as well that the relationships I formed didn't last. Looking back, I see they weren't the kind I'd do well to keep.

I hadn't pursued my dream to be a writer, the one Lenny had instilled in me nearly twenty years earlier. (I'll tell you all about that—and Lenny—later on.)

I had recently walked away from a job in a bakery in San Luis Obispo. The woman who owned the shop didn't like me much by then. I won't go into details, but I guess I don't blame her.

I'd given two weeks notice, but she relieved me of the two weeks. She got somebody else right away. And I'd been counting on having that two weeks' worth of income while I looked for another job. I had a nice new truck. I needed to keep up my payments.

I'd always worked, always made my own way, and I think this was a big part of my denial around drugs. It was my money, I worked hard for it. It was my time off, I'd earned it. If that was the way I wanted to spend it, who was to judge?

Now I had two choices. Take my scant funds and put them in the gas tank of my truck so I could go out and find work. Or buy more drugs. Which would run out. And then I'd have neither.

And to top it all off, I was going through a bad breakup.

It was a miserable time.

I decided, quite suddenly, after twenty years of self-medication, that I would just quit. I would just never do drugs again.

I decided this on a Friday afternoon.

That night I couldn't sleep. And I was out of coffee. You see, I'd been on the night shift at the bakery. And I hadn't managed to turn my sleep schedule around. And when I worked nights—especially in a bakery, where coffee is available and good—I tended to drink coffee by the pot, not by the cup. And caffeine withdrawal is hard.

It was early February, and it was cold. Unusually cold for my area of California. So cold that I was sleeping in the living room to be closer to the wood stove.

Except for that night, when I wasn't sleeping at all. It was almost 4:00 A.M., and I was wide awake.

I decided to walk across town (it's a small town, so the walk is a little less than two miles each way) to the local bakery where I had worked several years before. Because I vaguely knew the guy who did the morning donuts. And I knew I could sit and talk to him, and drink all the coffee I wanted.

It worked out fine … at first. I sat on a stool in the kitchen, near the warmth of the oven, talking to him and watching him work. Then he took out a pipe and asked me if I wanted to share some pot.

I said, "Sure." Or maybe I even said, "You bet." Or, "Hell, yeah."

I hadn't forgotten that I'd sworn off forever only hours before. I just didn't seem to know any other answers.

Strangely, as we smoked, we began to discuss our lives, and how they hadn't turned out the way we expected.

I asked him why he thought that was true, in the case of his own life.

He said, "Drugs. And some of the people I've taken up with."

And we passed the pipe.

He asked me what I thought had gone wrong in *my* life.

I said, "Drugs."

And still we passed the pipe.

In time I walked home, completely demoralized. My big pronouncement that I could quit drugs forever hadn't lasted half a day. Apparently I had a problem I didn't know how to solve. Me. The one who could always go it alone.

I got home, cleaned my room from top to bottom, took out the yellow pages, and looked up a number for a twelve-step program. I called. And was given two local numbers, one of which I also called. I spoke for nearly an hour to a woman who would become my first sponsor.

That night I attended my first meeting. It was a bit of a shock.

First I learned that alcohol was a drug, and I was also not supposed to drink. Then I was advised, "No new relationships in your first year."

I thought, *What have I gotten myself into?*

But I stayed. That was February 4, 1989. And I've been clean and sober since that day.

I think I might have stayed because of the woman who, after the meeting, told me, "Even if you get loaded, come back." I'd never heard anything like that before. I'd always found myself in places where I was only conditionally welcomed. I knew I was wanted in the meetings if I was clean and sober. If I was like them. The idea that they wanted to see me again regardless hit deep.

But that's not the real point of the story. This is:

My emotional pain at that moment was deep enough to drive me to change. That was my hitting bottom. If I could have mitigated it slightly, just like always, I would have. And then I'd still be limping along, like that. And none of the rest of the life I now know ever would have come to pass.

Sometimes I use hitting bottom as a reminder to the women I sponsor in the program. It's living proof that we don't really know the difference between a good thing and a bad thing when it's happening. Only much later.

I remind them of the miserable circumstances that brought them to recovery. They are, of course, in retrospect, not miserable at all. They are what brought them to recovery!

I can certainly sort my life into things I do and don't enjoy. But I really can't know what's good or bad. And it helps when I don't try.

Almost two years later I had another, similar experience.

I was laid off from a job, and it was the first job I'd ever really loved. I was working as a baker and pastry chef in a tiny local restaurant. The chef was my best friend, and no matter how busy we got, there was always harmony in the kitchen. I wanted to work there all my life. But in January of 1991, the restaurant went out of business. Which was the worst thing that could possibly have happened to me ... I thought.

There are very few jobs in a tourist town in January.

I sat down and wrote that novel I'd always said I would write, if I ever had the time.

I had the time.

And now I have a deep and abiding respect for the bad times in my life. If indeed they were ever bad.

In my novel *Chasing Windmills*, Delilah tells Sebastian, "Well, child, I'd tell you to be careful, except for two things. One, it wouldn't do any good anyhow. And two, I think we tell each other that too much. Be careful. Don't get hurt. Don't take chances. Don't try anything. Don't feel. Might as well be telling each other not to be alive at all. Boils down to the same thing."

Then she stands back and allows him to walk down an ill-advised path into a first love. He gets hurt. And ends up right where he needs to be.

As I say, if someone could have shown me how to take ten percent off the top of my misery, I would have just kept limping along. Without recovery. If I could have preserved that job, I would have.

So maybe we're on the right path after all. Even if it only looks right in our rearview mirror. Maybe we can trust what hindsight consistently shows.

Pinnacles

Cold Enough For You?

For more photos related to this story:
http://www.catherineryanhyde.com/the-long-steep-
path/pinnacles/

This is a story about paths that are cold, when it's warm inside. The kind of paths I'm often sorely tempted not to take.

I live close to Pinnacles National Monument. I feel fortunate in that regard. I can drive to Yosemite Valley in five and a half hours, and that never fails to delight. And I try to go often. But I can drive to Pinnacles National Monument in two hours. So I used to make it a point to hike there at least two or three times a year.

So why has it been more than two years since I've made the time?

Well, in summer, it's far too hot for me. Well over a hundred degrees. And in winter it's insanely cold, but that's no excuse. I can bundle up against the cold. And with the kind of climbing a hiker has to do on the Pinnacle trails, I'll warm up fast enough, anyway.

So, shortly after the New Year holiday, I'm giving it a go, complete with RV and an overnight stay.

Two good hikes are always better than one.

Now it's my second day, and a little after 8:00 A.M. Late for me to get out on the trail. In most cases, my goal is to plant my boots at the trailhead as soon as I can honestly say it's possible to see them moving down there. And even that might involve the use of a headlamp for the first forty-five minutes or so.

Today is a little different, because … it's … nippy.

As predicted, being January at Pinnacles National Monument, it's cold. How cold? I have a photo of a drip coming off a water spigot at the campground ... frozen solid. There's frost on the little wooden footbridges, and on the vegetation. Mud puddles on the trail are frozen into panes of varying sizes and shapes.

Yeah. You get the idea. It's cold.

And I live where it almost never is. So I'm not used to this kind of cold.

When it's that cold outside, some little voice inside me always says, *This bites. Let's go inside, where it's warm.*

But here's what I'm wondering this morning: *Is it always a good idea for me to listen?*

As I trudge along, I'm thinking about those who believe in the concept of nerve force. Truthfully, I'm not a hundred percent sure of all they mean by the phrase. But I have noticed the things people do to improve nerve force. For example, I know that's why the winter polar bear swims were invented. Ice-cold plunges are meant to foster nerve force.

So the bulk of my thoughts on the trail this morning have to do with nerve force, and its polar (no pun intended) opposite, comfort.

On a good day I enjoy comfort as much as the next person. On a bad one, perhaps more. And there's nothing wrong with that. To a point. But if in wanting comfort I seek it all the time ... Well, I do, occasionally. I call it "cocooning." And I try to be patient with myself about it, because I've learned that if I treat myself with patience, the need to cocoon passes on its own. But if I were to simply remain within my comfort zone, clinging to the way I want to feel—unchallenged—my comfort zone would just keep getting smaller.

Think about it. I sure did, and, oddly, I think maybe I never had before. The less I expose myself to cold weather, the more easily I will get cold, and the more I will be made miserable by it. So in seeking comfort in the short run, I'm actually making myself less comfortable in the long run. The more I endeavor always to be warm, the more I am insuring I will suffer from the cold.

Now, I'm not a polar bear. I don't jump into ice water, and I didn't set out on this frozen trail in a tee shirt. I have on a knit hat, gloves, a warm fleece.

But I did set out. And I'm uncomfortable.

The tips of my fingers ache right through my Polartec gloves. My face burns and my ears sting. I'm having to make seven unbridged creek crossings (in each direction), being ever so careful not to slip off the rocks and plant a foot deeper than the tops of my waterproof boots. One does not want a boot full of freezing creek water on a thirty-degree morning.

Part of me wants only to go back inside the RV, where it's warm. Where I could turn on the furnace, and make hot tea and hot soup. But I keep hiking, and the feeling begins to fade. I warm up from the inside. I'm moving, working, and that creates its own heat.

In time the sun rises up over the mountain and shines on my back. And I appreciate it. The sun shines on me every day. But this morning I feel it, I focus on it, and I am grateful for it.

Three-plus hours and seven miles later I return to the RV, which is, by now, plenty warm enough without the furnace. I make hot tea and hot soup. And, I guarantee you, I enjoy it more than I would have if I'd wimped out on the cold-but-spectacular hike. Now I feel like I've earned it. I stepped outside my comfort level and experienced a morning of joy.

In my humble and exhausted opinion, joy beats comfort every time.

And that is my brief reflection on the subject of comfort and joy. I've decided I'll take the joy.

Glacier Point

Do What You Said You'd Do

For more photos related to this story:
http://www.catherineryanhyde.com/the-long-steep-
path/glacier-point/

Ayear ago autumn I had to cancel a Yosemite hike at the very last minute. I'd really been looking forward to that hike, too. Kind of broke my heart. If I'd had a bit more time to adjust, I expect I'd have gotten over it easily enough. But I had already driven to Yosemite National Park with my mom and my dog (they have fun just being in the valley while I take my day-long hikes). I had already checked in to my reserved campsite with the little motor home. I already had a one-way ticket for the bus up to Glacier Point.

I was … *so ready.*

I knew it might rain. I'd seen that in the weather reports as the time grew nearer. And, you know what? I didn't care. When I'm really looking forward to a hike, I'll walk in just about anything nature wants to dish out.

Here's the hike I was so looking forward to doing: I was going to take the bus tour—one-way only—up to Glacier Point, 3,200 feet over Yosemite Valley, and then hike the Panorama Trail back down to my campsite.

I knew it was supposed to be an amazing trail. Just eye-poppingly scenic. On the high trail, close to Glacier Point, you're looking down over Vernal and Nevada Falls from thousands of feet above. Later in the hike, you're trekking down the trails right beside them. Right in their blowing mist. The trail also takes you over Illouette Creek for a good view of Illouette Fall, one of the few Yosemite waterfalls I had never seen.

It was the day before the hike, and it was raining. A lot.

I started thinking maybe just my little cheap plastic emergency poncho (the kind that comes folded up to the size of a big wallet) might not be all I'd want. I hopped the shuttle, rode into the village, and bought a proper poncho.

My pack was full. My water bladder had been filled with sports drink. I had snacks in my pack. I had my hiking clothes all laid out.

I went to sleep.

And woke to the sound of thunder. Close thunder. A lightning storm had descended on Yosemite.

Now, I said a minute ago that I would walk in whatever nature wanted to dish out. May I back up now and add an exception? Thank you. Anything except lightning. Rain doesn't tend to kill hikers dead. Lightning has that unfortunate tendency. When hiking in the high country, lightning cancels. That is a hard and fast rule. That's one you don't want to play around with. Not if you want to live to hike another day.

I swallowed my disappointment, and we drove home. I vowed there would be a makeup hike in my future.

Now it's October of the following year, and I'm here in Yosemite for my make-up hike. And a lot has changed in one year. I'm in much better shape. I have a two-night reservation at Phantom Ranch (at the bottom of the Grand Canyon) that I've been holding onto for nearly a year. Which means I'm going to be hiking into and out of the Grand Canyon less than two months from today. So I've been training very hard.

So ... none of that riding up on a bus nonsense. I'm going to hike from camp all the way up to Glacier Point, 3,200 vertical feet above the valley floor. But it's actually a hike with a 3,900-foot elevation gain, because the Panorama Trail loses 700 feet on its way down to Illouette Creek. And, as any good peak hiker knows, what goes down must come up. So that elevation has to be regained on the other side of the creek. So 3,900 feet ... that's about 500 feet less than the climb out of the Grand Canyon.

Good practice for me.

Here's the only question that lingered in my head during the planning. Would I also hike the Four-Mile Trail back down into the valley?

Usually that's pretty much a given. You hike up to the top of something high, it's more or less mandatory that you hike it back down. But Glacier Point is served by busses.

Here's what I decided: No bus. I'd hike it back down. The simple deciding factor was this: there would be no bus to take me down to the river at the Grand Canyon. Steep downhill is hard, too. Downhill muscles also need good training.

I decided to do the whole thing on foot.

Now it's hike morning. Very early. In fact, it's still dark. I know it's going to be a little on the hot side today, so I purposely planned to take off in the dark, by headlamp.

Not a creature is stirring. I hope. My fellow campers are all asleep.

This is when I have that flash of doubt. This is where my brain says, "Do I really want to do this? 3,900 feet? On foot? I'm purposely choosing something this hard as a way to spend my day?"

I've got to tell you, this is where social networking comes in handy. This is when it pays to have told a couple of thousand people what you plan to do. What would I tweet next, if for some reason I froze and didn't get my butt out the door? "Not quite in the mood after all"?

But I *am* in the mood (sort of … in there somewhere) and I *am* going to do it. It's just that moment of doubt. It's that message from my self-preservation instinct. Today it says, *Just so you know … you're about to go out into a dark wilderness inhabited by bears and the occasional mountain lion. Okay, that's all. Just making sure you hadn't forgotten.*

I honor that voice in me. There's always a twinge of fear before a huge hike. There should be. If I plunged into that type of adventure without the slightest twinge of fear, I'd consider it a sign that I shouldn't be allowed out there. Because it would mean I didn't truly comprehend the task ahead.

I proceed to do what I said I would do.

I step out.

It's really quiet. And really dark.

I can't even see the Merced River as I climb the steep, paved trail alongside it. I can only hear it. The wind is blowing, strangely gusty for predawn. It feels inhospitable.

And I'm a little too dizzy and out of breath.

Now, that last part is a problem.

I sit on a rock and wonder what's up. It's a month after my hike on Pike's Peak. So it can't be that I'm not in shape for it. And that was at elevations of about 6,500 to over 10,000 feet. This starts at 4,000 and goes up to about 7,200. And I'm still down around 4,000. So it's not that the altitude is getting to me.

I get up and trudge a little more.

I think about what my mom told me before I left the motor home. She said she hadn't slept well. That she'd been awake with a feeling like her throat was closing up.

It hits me then: there's something here in the valley that's causing an allergic reaction.

Of course. That makes perfect sense.

I puff my way up to the footbridge over the river. The sky is just barely light now. I can look upriver and see Vernal Fall looming above me in the dim.

I search through my fairly thoughtfully filled pack and find exactly one nondrowsy antihistamine.

One is all I need.

Forty-five minutes later, I'm a few hundred feet higher, on the John Muir Trail, and doing a bit better. Better than I would be if I hadn't taken an antihistamine, anyway. But not as well as I'd be doing if I weren't allergic.

Whatever. Okay, so it's a slightly off day. So now my job is to do what I said I'd do even though it's an off day.

Here's the thing about doing what I said I'd do. I've mentioned it a couple of times, and now I'm going to tell you why I think it's so important.

Have you ever known one of those people who always tell you these great things they're going to do … but then they never do them? Probably not. That is, probably not one. You've probably known several.

It's like the boy who cried wolf. After awhile you hear them talking about another great thing they're going to do, and you think, *No, you won't. You never do.*

We have that same reaction to ourselves, too. If we observe that we often don't do what we say we'll do, we start not to believe a single word we say.

So I give myself that advice a lot on the trail. I use it as a reminder, not as a bayonet at my back. There's just always this tendency to think, *Whoa. The summit still looks a long way up. Maybe I should just hike up to that ridge and call it a day.* It's a coin that could land either way. So I just give it a little nudge by saying, *No, do what you said you'd do.*

And, almost without exception, I do.

Now I'm trudging my way up the last part of the trail, just a mile or so under Glacier Point. It's hot (for me). I'm tired. I mean, really first class, you'll-remember-this-feeling-for-a-long-time tired. Every ten steps or so I have to stop for a few beats. Get up the energy to take ten more.

But it really is amazing. I have to say. I can look down and see not only Half Dome in relief, but Vernal and Nevada Falls so far below me that they just look like vertical strips of white. I'm so high above them that I can't even tell that it's flowing water. I started out my morning having to climb up many hundreds of feet to reach the falls, and now they're so far below me that I can't see the moving water.

Hopefully now you get why I'm so tired.

I start to think about that bus.

When I get up to the parking lot, there will likely be a bus sitting there. Maybe I should stick my head in and ask the driver if he has an empty seat. Buy myself a ride back down.

I decide it's an option I should be allowed to keep in my back pocket.

When I get up there, it's crowded. There are hundreds of people milling about. And the bus is there. Idling. It's loud. It stinks of exhaust fumes. And I know it's not what I came out here to do. In fact, it doesn't even look appealing.

I follow the sign to the Four-Mile Trail, and begin the hike down.

I look out across the valley and realize I'm looking down at the top of Upper Yosemite Fall. Now, I ask you ... how often does one get to look *down* at Upper Yosemite Fall?

And, you know what? I'm really not as tired as I thought. I was just tired of climbing *up*.

So now I climb down. Just like I said I would do.

But Don't Ask Too Much of Yourself

The Grand Canyon in a Winter Storm

Don't Do What You Said You'd Do

Speaking of hikes getting cancelled at the last minute…

This one's a real heartbreaker for me.

I secured these aforementioned Phantom Ranch reservations last December. For this December. Phantom Ranch reservations are not easy to get. I waited *a year*.

I trained all year.

I bought extra supplies, like a backpacker stove (my multiple food allergies make it impossible for me to rely on the Phantom Ranch meals) and gaiters to keep any potential high snow out of my boots.

I put my pack together a month in advance. Yes, a month. I don't know … because I'm crazy, that's why. I Tweeted and Facebooked, "Does it make me a total freak that my pack is already loaded up for the Grand Canyon trip?" Even my better friends had to concede that, yes, it more or less did. But I was that excited.

I drove from the Central Coast of California to the South Rim, after a couple of other stops in the area.

I'd been watching the Grand Canyon weather for a long time. Watching the possibility of precipitation get higher, then lower. Then higher again. Then shift days a bit.

Now I'm here at the Canyon, where it's bitterly cold (but what do you expect on the last day of November?), checking in at the Bright Angel Transportation

Desk. I reference their posted weather. The forty percent chance of rain/snow for tomorrow, my hike-in day, has gone to ninety percent. The day after that, the in-the-canyon day that I plan to spend hiking the North Kaibab Trail to Ribbon Falls, the chance of rain stands at forty percent. The day I hike out—by far the most important day for good weather—is only showing a slight chance of bad weather.

And … oh, yeah. Wind. There will be lots of wind.

No more pretending it's just a light snow flurry or a bit of a rain shower. This is a winter storm. The only real question now is how severe a winter storm it plans to become.

I ask the woman at the desk if the rangers ever advise people not to go down. Because I promised myself (and a few others) that if the rangers called the timing inadvisable, I wouldn't go.

She says, "No, they don't tell you not to go. Just to be prepared."

Oh. They don't *ever* tell you not to go. So that wasn't going to be my litmus test after all.

We go over my preparations.

I tell her I have a rain poncho (okay, so what if it says Yosemite National Park on it?—it still works), gaiters, good trekking poles, and instep crampons to use in the event of an icy trail.

She asks if I have a good warm hat.

I say yes, I have an Air Core ski hat and gloves.

She says it sounds like I'm ready. Like I know what I'm getting myself into. Those aren't her exact words, but, let's face it, that's what they really want to know about you.

I check in at the campground. And wait.

I'm seized by an unfortunate thought.

How will I eat?

As I mentioned, I can't eat the food at Phantom Ranch. I checked, when I first made the reservation. They serve two or three basic meals, the same for everybody who wants to eat there. I had the reservation agent read me the meal ingredients over the phone. And every single one contains something I'm allergic to.

If you're going to get sick with food allergies, it's really best to do so in your own home.

Or close to home.

Or someplace closer to help.

Or really any place that isn't the absolute bottom of the freaking Grand Canyon.

So I've brought my own home-dehydrated backpacker meals, and a little stove.

Except you can't use those stoves indoors. The fumes could kill somebody.

You also can't use them outside in the whipping rain.

I call the desk again to see if the food service people at Phantom Ranch would provide hot water in a pinch.

I get my answer.

Absolutely not.

Apparently the people who are camping across the creek, and the people who want to save money by not buying meals, come in with a lot of requests. So the policy is quite strict.

Okay, another question. While I have her on the phone. Is there any place at or near Phantom Ranch that is outdoors, but covered?

She puts me on hold, talks to a supervisor, then comes back and tells me that, to the best of both of their memories, there is no such place.

Now I have a big decision to make.

I decide it's safe to chance it, provided I beef up my store of trail mix and pack one more almond butter sandwich. That will cover me in a pinch. I can eat all fresh food on the first day. And on the second day there's only a forty percent chance of precipitation (snow on the rim, where it's cold; rain at the river, where's it's more like Phoenix weather). So sixty percent of the time it should be good for cooking … er … rehydrating. Right?

I repack slightly, and lay out the clothes I'll wear.

Then, somehow, I manage to get some sleep.

When I wake up, it's still not snowing yet. I make a cup of tea. I'm not in a big hurry, since all I'm doing this first day is hiking in.

I decide to check the weather one more time on my little smartphone.

What was last night ninety percent, followed by forty percent, followed by "slight chance " has progressed overnight. It is now ninety, ninety, ninety. It's going to be bad weather every single one of those three days. And conditions seem to be falling apart fast.

I picture myself hiking out of the Canyon in a big winter storm. High winds pushing me back. If the temperature is in the thirties, I'll be in freezing rain. My gloves are not waterproof. The wind may be pushing freezing rain under my poncho, which might be blowing so hard it can't fully protect me. Those last three miles—everything between the three-mile rest house and the rim—are the toughest hiking I have ever done. They are so hard that I just can't imagine anything making them even five percent harder. And I've been warned that this part of the trail will be muddy. I picture mud balls forming on my boots. Weighing them down. Needing to be scraped off every two-dozen steps.

And of course I won't have had enough to eat.

It's a six- to seven-hour trek for me in good conditions.

I'll pause here to note that I hike for the joy of it. Not because I want to put myself through hour after hour of living hell.

I call the desk again. Get the same woman. Tell her I'm calling it. I'm not going down. I figure, since I'm already checked in and all, that they'll want to know.

I drive out of camp and cruise along Desert View Drive to a good vantage point. Eat breakfast and watch the storm blow in over the Canyon. For a bit too long, really. As I'm driving away from the park, I realize I should have gotten a better head start on the storm. Driving in a winter storm can create problems, too.

By the time I get to Williams and the I-40 West, it's snowing heavily.

The highway rises in elevation, and the snow gets deeper. Comes down harder. Soon a line of cars are carefully following in each other's tire tracks in the right-hand lane at about thirty miles under the speed limit. Nobody wants to pass because the left lane doesn't have tire tracks.

The snow doesn't turn to rain until I'm ten miles outside of Kingman, Arizona.

Then I'm assaulted with high winds, and I hunker down in Barstow and sleep the night, rather than risk being blown off the road.

I try to call home, to check on my dog Ella and my mom, but I get no answer and no answering machine. I call my across-the-street neighbor on her cell phone, and find out that everyone's fine, that she's just been over to my house to check on my mom, but that the power is out due to forty-seven-miles-per-hour winds.

I update my status from my phone:

> Shouldn't have sat at the rim watching weather blow in just because it looks cool. Should have tried to beat the storm out. Feel like I barely made it.

> Buckets of snow on the I-40 from Williams to almost Kingman. Not much more fun to drive in this storm than it would have been to hike in it.

> Just barely back into CA, and man that wind is howling.

> Back in CA, the weather is better. Just not by much.

I arrive home tired and painfully disappointed, but also knowing that, even for all my cautions, I might not have taken that storm seriously enough.

The morning of that hike day would not have been a good moment to tell myself to do what I said I would do. I said I'd hike into the Grand Canyon, not that I'd battle a storm into it. When the situation changed, I had to change, too.

I can mope all I want, but that's never very useful. Besides, time to get back to my #DailyGratitude. (More about that as I continue. But for now, just know that every day I post one thing for which I am grateful on all my social networking sites.)

Here's what I post, all in one day:

> Time for #DailyGratitude. I'm sure you all know I'm bummed that I got "weathered out" of my Canyon hike by a Winter storm. Still …

> At all times I was warm, dry, fed and safe. #DailyGratitude

> I got to visit Hopiland and meet a couple of the people there, and I had a great day in Sedona with my friend Abby. #DailyGratitude

> The Canyon hasn't gone anywhere, so I can always try again. (Plus it would have been my 4th time, so have seen it.) #DailyGratitude

Hiking Junipero Serra tomorrow. Not the same scenery, but a workout similar to hiking out of the Canyon. #DailyGratitude

But, you know what? I have a weird outcome to report. I only hike about three-quarters of Junipero Serra. Because that's what feels right. I know I can make it all the way up if I need to. But … I don't.

If I'd been coming up out of the Canyon, I'd need to. I'd have no choice. The thing is … I'm not coming up out of the Canyon. I had just somehow made up my mind that I *ought to* take a hike with equivalent elevation. I don't *need* to do that much. And it suddenly strikes me to question whether I *want* to.

I've climbed a good 2,700 feet, and this voice in the back of my head is saying, *Isn't this fitness? It feels like fitness.*

Maybe that's failing to do what I said I would do. But in this case, I don't think so. I think it's that sanity I referred to earlier. Kicking in at long last.

Can't Be What Everybody Wants Me To Be

Some Very Brief Thoughts About Speaking Up

I tend to think of myself as someone who speaks my mind fairy easily. So I've been quite surprised by my recent foray into a whole new realm of truth telling. I don't mean truth telling as opposed to lying, because I haven't indulged in outright lying in years. I mean as opposed to keeping quiet about how I feel.

I'm talking about speaking up.

Turns out I'm not nearly as good at it as I thought.

Not everyone is pleased by hearing my truth. I guess there's no such thing as a world in which you can say what you mean and enjoy everyone's approval. And that, I think, is the real bottom line on speaking up.

I guess it just boils down to this one key question: How much do I care what others think of me?

More than I thought, I guess. But I'm doing it anyway. Because once you pull the covers off a pattern like that, there's just no going home again.

One major observation did break through is this regard: I realized that I used to want to be liked and respected by everybody. Now I want to be liked and respected by the people I like and respect. This is both a more achievable and, in my opinion, a more healthy goal.

Though it's not the most dramatic recent example, today two people—two total strangers—emailed me for the first time ever and asked me to mail them a free book. One was in Russia, the other in Brazil. Ever mailed a parcel to Russia or Brazil? It's not cheap.

Now, there was a time when I could have absorbed that expense quite easily. But even so, one has to wonder why I would say yes to these two people and not everybody else, and how I would absorb the expense if I were to apply this favor fairly and evenly across the board. Well, I couldn't, of course. Everybody has to draw the line somewhere. Sometime.

So why procrastinate?

I did something I almost never do in this situation. I said, with regrets, that I could not.

Maybe I'm still weighed down with the burden of being that *Pay It Forward* person. She has to be nice, right? But *Paying It Forward* is about spontaneously offering favors, not needing to say yes when someone asks too much of you. And also, it's about kindness rather than niceness. There's a difference. Kindness is spontaneous and real. Niceness just mostly wants to be liked.

Many years ago, when I lived in L.A., there was a little mom-and-pop store on the corner. Behind the register was a hand-done sign. Here's what it said:

YOU ASK FOR CREDIT, I SAY NO, YOU GET MAD
I GIVE YOU CREDIT, YOU DON'T PAY, I GET MAD
BETTER YOU GET MAD

Life is full of moments when two people's needs are in conflict. Someone is going to be unhappy. If I speak up, it will be the other person. If I don't, it will be me.

I guess I'm wondering why I spent all those years choosing me.

Half Dome, Yosemite

I Know It With My Knower

For more photos related to this story:
http://www.catherineryanhyde.com/the-long-steep-
path/half-dome/

Several years ago, I took on Half Dome as a day hike. I'd just come off my first day hike of the Grand Canyon, south rim to river to south rim. I figured if I could do that, I could do anything.

I was not entirely correct.

Mostly. But not entirely.

I made it up nearly eight miles of tough trail, including the Thousand Stairs to the base of Half Dome's cables, despite the eighty-five-degree heat. (For me, that's extreme weather.) I made it despite the fact that earlier in the hike I'd chosen the "stairs" beside Vernal Fall, because I'd never seen the waterfall before. (And all together that's a lot of granite step-ups.) Despite the fact that, as is so often the case, no one I knew was willing to bite off a day hike of this ferocity. I was going it solo.

A dark cloud could have stopped me in my boots, because Half Dome is famous for lightning strikes. But the sky was perfect blue.

I was on track to succeed.

I donned the leather gloves I'd brought just for the purpose, and started up the infamous cable ascent.

I didn't make it.

I'd set aside days for the trip to Yosemite, planned, trained, and sweated my way up about ninety-nine percent of the trail to the top. But I never stood on the very top of Half Dome. And I don't expect I ever will.

Why? Because I was in over my head. And I knew it.

First, the rock is slippery. Even when dry. It's worn smooth, and the traction is not good. See, I thought I'd be standing solidly, if at a slant, mostly using my hands for balance.

Sometimes the path is not what I imagined. Sometimes I don't really know the scope of the challenges until I meet them. Until I hit them (hopefully figuratively) head-on.

And another issue: because the rock was so slick, you could only rest—even for a moment—at the wooden two-by-four crosspieces that bisected the "trail" at each post. Several were missing. So I had to make it twice as far on arm strength alone.

Upper body strength is my weakness.

Then I looked up and saw two crosspieces missing. In a row.

I watched a much younger couple struggle mightily to cover that difficult gap.

That's when I made a mistake. As I let go of the cable with my left hand, I allowed myself to overbalance backward. Just a little. Just for a split second. But it was a wake-up call.

I caught myself. Of course. Pulled hard with my right and managed to get balanced again. If I hadn't, I wouldn't be writing this. But I looked up to the top. And I wondered how tired my arms would be by the time I got up there. And if I might overbalance again. And if I'd have enough remaining strength to right myself.

Then I looked down. Behind me. And I knew that another mistake could be my last.

I backed down. Literally.

I lowered myself backward on the cables until I was down. And, as I trudged the many hours back down the mountain, alone, I struggled against the tendency to second-guess my decision.

It helped a little (but not enough) to go over my hiking priorities. They are as follows:

1. Survive to hike another day.
2. Come down off the mountain on my own two feet, not in a Medevac helicopter.
3. Have fun out there.
4. Summit.

See? Summiting isn't even in the top three.

So why was I so disappointed?

Partly because I'd wanted so badly to reach that summit. Partly because I felt as though I *should* have been able to. But the truth is not that I was literally unable. The truth is that it would not have been wise (for me, personally) to keep trying. And I knew it.

How could I be so sure?

As my old and dear friend Pat, now deceased, used to say, "I know it with my knower."

Pat said many wise things, and I'll tell you a lot more about her before I'm done. She more than warrants her own inspirational story. She was living, breathing inspiration when she was living.

Maybe in some ways she still is.

But I can't get through this story without just that one Pat quote:

"I know it with my knower."

Until I was well-acquainted with my knower, I knew only to look for it somewhere between my heart and my lower intestines, to trust it to tell me the truth whenever I consulted it, and to try valiantly to get through to me even when I didn't.

Now we're on much closer and more personal terms.

If I'm just tired and wanting to do less, I figure maybe my answer is to push myself a little harder. But if I'm in over my head, I know it's time to back down.

Like the Serenity Prayer, the tricky part is having the wisdom to know the difference.

So here are some photos of the astonishing Half Dome. But they were not shot from the top. Because some risks are not worth taking.

I know that with my knower.

Pike's Peak

Promises, Promises

For more photos related to this story:
http://www.catherineryanhyde.com/the-long-steep-
path/pikes-peak-hike/

In the two days before my mom and I boarded the Pike's Peak Cog Railway, which I will tell you more about as I go along, I took another big hike. Not as big as it could have been. Not as big as past hikes. Not as big as that naggy little voice at the back of my head says it should have been. But by any reasonable standard, it was pretty big.

It was the bottom half of Pike's Peak.

I hiked up the Barr Trail to Barr Camp, which is 6.5 miles and 3,800 vertical feet, (each way) or a little better than half the way to Pike's Peak summit.

I'd had the night's reservation for Barr Camp for a long time. The better part of a year. I spent that time wrestling with myself about the summit.

I had two choices. I could hike up to Barr Camp, spend a night in the fall aspens, and hike back down the next day. Then the day after that I could take my mom up to the summit on the cog railway.

Second option, I could spend one night at Barr Camp, then hike to the summit, hopefully in time to meet my mom and her train, so I could get the ride back down.

Here's the problem, though. The second option would have been breaking a promise to myself.

When I was up on the Inca Trail to Machu Picchu, as I've reported to you in much detail, I hiked up over

14,000 feet for the first time ever. Also the last time ever.

I made a promise to myself on the aptly named Dead Woman's Pass: no more 14,000-footers. I live at sea level, and, though I didn't get mountain sickness (amazingly, I didn't even get a headache), I couldn't breathe. Even when standing still. And when you can't catch your breath standing still, trudging up multiple miles and thousands of feet of elevation is a trial, to say the least.

So I made a vow to myself. From now on, I'm sticking to around 10,000 feet.

Then along came Pike's Peak. And how negotiable that promise became!

I flip-flopped a number of times, but ended up taking the position that a promise is a promise. It was made for a good reason. Had I gone for the summit, I don't doubt that the reason would have become painfully clear. But I didn't. I hiked the 6.5 miles and 3,800 feet (about 600 feet short of climbing out of the Grand Canyon) and it was enough.

A couple of years ago, when I was composing the text for the "About Me" page of my website, I explained the change in my hiking by saying I'm trying to be fit but not insane.

So far so good.

Most promises seem to go the opposite direction. I'll go faster, I'll go higher, I'll achieve something I've never achieved before. But there's nothing wrong with a promise to save yourself unnecessary discomfort.

There was a time when I felt I needed to prove things to myself. To prove I could dayhike the Grand

Canyon, that I could get over the Knife Edge on Mt. Katahdin, that I could hike from Yosemite Valley to Cloud's Rest and back in one day. Having done that, a trip to the summit of Pike's Peak would beg the question, What am I trying to prove now, and to whom?

Besides, I knew I'd be taking a trip to the summit, the day after I hiked down, with my eighty-nine-year-old mom.

There's more than one way to get up a mountain.

Let the People Around
You Inspire and Direct
and Help and Change
You

Lenny

The Opposite of What I Can't Do

Here's the second most common question I receive: "What inspired you to become a writer?"

Here's the answer I give:

He wasn't a what. He was a who.

He was Lenny.

There is no way I can define myself as a writer without mentioning Lenny Horowitz, my high school English teacher. I never called him Mr. Horowitz. He let us call him Lenny.

Lenny sent my world in a completely different direction. And before you finish this book, you will have at least a glimpse of where I was headed at the time. The more you read, the more I think you'll understand and agree that he was a lifesaver.

Here's what Lenny did to save me: He taught me to love reading again. And he told me I could write.

When I was little, nobody had to teach me to love reading. Books were water; I was a duck. I pitched into *Dr. Seuss*, *Winnie the Pooh*, the *Black Stallion* series. I was unstoppable. My friend Mary Jo and I even staged our own two-kid contests, sitting in the library all day and racing to see who could read more picture books at one sitting.

When my parents called "lights out," I was the kid under the covers, finishing my book quietly by flashlight.

This is passion that can't be taught. Encouraged. But not taught.

Then came school, where my irresistible force met an immovable object. I hated the books I was given to read. They didn't speak to me. They were almost as bad as—I hate to even utter the dreaded word—homework.

I began to avoid reading if possible. I honed the talent of writing book reports on books I hadn't read.

To this day, I have a chip on my shoulder about the classic-classics. I've tried twice to read *Moby-Dick*. I give up. I'm not ashamed, either. I like modern, fast-moving fiction. I've taken my last run at the great white whale. Ever. It's over.

Back to Lenny.

He gave us different books to read. Books like *Bless the Beasts and Children*, and *Flowers for Algernon*, modern classics that remain among my favorites to this day. I never would have known about those books if not for Lenny. And another all-time favorite, *Of Mice and Men*, which is as close to the actual classics as I get with that "passion that can't be taught" intact.

And he introduced us to plays, like *Twelve Angry Men* and *A Raisin in the Sun*.

I have no idea if anybody else in the class even noticed, or cared. I don't know what my peers thought of these books and plays. I probably didn't have a good enough relationship with them to ask, and I'm sure I didn't understand them well enough to figure it out on my own.

I was an involuntary island in high school. Or maybe a partially voluntary one. I'm not sure.

I only know what Lenny meant to *me*.

Lenny was a mere ten years older than we were. About twenty-four to my fourteen. And the books he assigned reflected that. These were books written in the same century he assigned them. Books with down-and-out characters, people outside the mainstream. I understood these people. *I* was outside the mainstream. I was overweight and had braces on my teeth. My peer group thought I was from outer space. I liked reading about characters on the margins. We had something in common.

Miracle of miracles, I woke up.

One day Lenny gave out a creative writing assignment: an essay, on any subject. I still remember how he walked up to the blackboard and wrote, in big block letters: I AIN'T TAKING IT AFTER FRIDAY.

Not exactly your run-of-the-mill English teacher, right?

I was so impressed by his willingness to meet us where we lived that I decided to impress him back.

I wrote an essay intended to be funny. Always risky. It was a takeoff on the my-dog-ate-my-homework excuse note, a long, rambling, slapstick story explaining why I was not able to hand in my essay on time.

Sight unseen, Lenny read it out loud in front of the class.

Decades later, I still remember the key line of dialogue. I'm fictionally running up the down escalator at the airport, chasing the guy who picked up the wrong briefcase and is about to get on a plane with my essay. "But Mr. Malenkiowitz," I shout plaintively, "you don't understand. He ain't taking it after Friday!"

They laughed. Everybody, including Lenny. They laughed a lot. For a long time. It was my first whiff of the rare smell of success.

Lenny told the class my essay was clever. Later I found out he was still talking about it in the staff lounge that day. He told all my other teachers I could write.

If I'd been used to praise at school, it might not have had such an impact. But I was that kid who got picked last for basketball. And dating, well … I'd rather not talk about dating. I was used to being told what I couldn't do. What I could do was more of a mystery. Until Lenny spoke.

Unfortunately, Lenny was diagnosed with Hodgkin's disease in my junior year. I went on to follow everything but my dream for two more decades, mostly alcohol and drugs, and relationships that brought nothing but pain. And I was diligent in those pursuits. Until I finally stopped, I was unstoppable. But my real dream, to be a writer, was misclassified as a wish until I was in my midthirties.

By the time I became a for-real writer, it was too late to go back and tell him what he'd done. All I have for Lenny is the tribute. So I offer tributes to Lenny as often as opportunities present themselves.

Here's what I learned from Lenny in my sophomore year of high school: the down-and-out character is just as human as everybody else. You may not want to know him in real life, but in fiction, you just might dare. And in knowing him, you get a lesson in humanity: we're more the same than we might imagine.

And that even the class outcast has talents. Some-one just needs to tell her what they are.

The class outcast, I can attest, will (eventually) take it from there.

Jean

One Good Mentor

The trails at Grand Canyon and Joshua Tree I walked alone. The path to publication I did not. Nor could I have. I needed mentorship.

My first true mentor was author Jean Brody (*Gideon's House, A Coven of Women, Cleo*). I met her when I first had the guts to join the Cambria Writers Workshop and read my work out loud. Picture if you will: hands trembling as they try to hold the printout, hammering heart, much pausing for life-giving oxygen.

She wasn't an easy or soft mentor. In fact, I once stayed away from the group in despair when she announced that all my authority figures came off as stereotypes. I respected her knowledge so much that I allowed it to crush me.

Why did I go back? Because I got a phone call from a group member, asking if I'd left because I wasn't getting the kind of help I needed. She went on to say that I was doing good work and she'd hate to see me drop away.

Want to venture a guess?

Right. Jean Brody.

So I returned, and learned a lesson about hearing criticism.

Jean Brody owned and operated the Cambria Book Company, a small independent shop in Cambria's

West Village. So if I needed mentorship, I knew where to find it. And what better place than a bookstore?

In the window she kept a selection of books by local authors. Under the glass of the counter were great cartoons related to the book business. The shelf that comprised the front of the counter held recommended reads, books that Jean felt her customers would love. And behind the counter, a rack of special orders waited for her special readers.

I'd bring in my rejection slips, especially if I found them confusing.

"What did he *mean* by that?" I'd wail, reading aloud the editor's cryptic comment.

"Oh, it's all nonsense," she'd say. "Pay no attention to any of it."

"Why do I keep banging my head against this wall?"

"You have to be crazy. You just have to be crazy for this line of work."

"Oh. That's good, I guess," I'd say, feeling a little better. "Since I'm obviously not outgrowing it, it's nice to finally be in a line of work where it's considered a plus."

Sometimes I'd read a novel or a story that was so good that it made me doubt myself and my own work. I'd bring it in to Jean and say, "I couldn't have done this!"

"No," she'd say. "You do something different."

A mere 122 rejection slips later, I began to publish some stories. How did I weather so many rejections without giving up?

That's probably the third most common question I'm asked.

Mentorship.

I didn't give up because authors like Jean Brody and Sherry Shahan and Elizabeth Spurr were right there, telling me, "This happens to all writers. You're good enough. It's right around the corner for you." Without that, 122 rejections seem to be saying, "Don't quit your day job." I needed someone who spoke in a louder voice.

Within a few years, I was one of the local authors with books in the window, and the special order shelf behind the counter held copies of my books, to be signed and inscribed by me before pick-up. Jean would call me when she had such an order, and I'd make it a point to drop by.

Then Jean moved to Northern California, and the little Cambria Book Company was no more. Now there's a bead shop in its place, which was very handy when I broke the wire on a beloved bracelet. But, waiting for it to be restrung, I deeply missed the little bookstore.

In early 2011, I received word that Jean had passed away.

It was interesting and enlightening to read the memories of her, posted by friends in her online guest book. One thing for sure, I was not remembering her wrong. She was much beloved, but she was in no way sweet. She was the kind of person to whom my mom would apply the brief description, "Doesn't suffer fools gladly."

Case in point, I remembered her response to the old saw, "Everyone has at least one book in them." Jean cried, without hesitation, "But God forbid they should all write it!"

Jean was not famous for telling people what they wanted to hear. I realized that Jean rarely, if ever, gave me just the words I'd hoped for.

So, I asked myself, *can a person inspire me by telling me what I hope to hear?* I'm thinking not. Unless I want someone to inspire me to stay the same.

I don't. I want more mentors like Jean.

Even more importantly, I want to *be* a mentor like Jean. Well. Not exactly like her. I do something different. But I strive to reward good creative high jumping by raising the bar even higher.

That, to me, is the heart and soul of *Paying It Forward*.

Inspiration by Negative Example

A Letter to My Late Friend

Dear You,

I'm writing this to you directly, in the second person, because it doesn't seem right to use your name. So I won't. I'll just call you, you.

It's hard for me to believe it's been six and a half years already. It doesn't feel that long. I wonder how your family must feel today, if it's still so real and immediate to me.

I still remember exactly where in my house I was standing when I got the call from our mutual friend. I remember who it was, and what words she used.

I remember clicking off the phone and just staring at it. Letting it sit limply in my hand, and watching it. First as if things might make sense if I gave them more time. Then as if I could force the words that had just come through that handset to justify themselves to me.

I had two friends over, visiting, when I got the call. I rejoined them and told them that a friend, someone I really cared about, had just taken his own life. They were concerned. But the path of their lives seemed to go forward.

I guess I shouldn't have expected anything more. They didn't know you. I did.

The path of my life did not go forward. Not quite that easily. Not for a long while.

I remembered sitting in meetings with you while you never shared about depression. Never uttered the word, as best I can recall.

I shared about it. Some. My depression was better by then, but it still came around to visit. Still does, to this very day, but not as often, and it doesn't stay as long.

I was having some breakthroughs about depression in those meetings with you. I was starting to be able to tell the difference between it and me. I was able to start saying, "I'm having some depression." As in, here I am, and some depression is here with me as well. Which was a big improvement over saying, "I am depressed." Which is almost like saying, "I am depression."

I'm not, as it turns out.

This was right around the time I was learning that the advice people give you when you're depressed is unhelpful and wrong. At least for me.

They say, "Get up, cheer up. Snap out of it. Go help somebody, go think about something else."

I had begun to reject the idea that distraction cures depression. I had begun to give it what it asked for. To take a big, deep breath, hold my nose, and sink all the way down to the bottom of that pool.

Know why? Yes, I know you do. Because when I talked about it, I remember you always nodded. But I didn't remember those nods until later. Until after you were gone.

Because in three or five or seven days, I'd always float back up closer to the surface again. And that episode would be over. Really over. That's why. But I'm saying this more for the sake of others (though I don't claim it's good advice for anybody else but me). Not so much for you. Because you already know.

Why didn't you give it more time?

I guess it doesn't help to be mad at you. But it also doesn't help to pretend I'm not.

I got mad at you a lot in that first year. I remember one of the times I went to sit by your grave. And I read the stone. For maybe the thirtieth time. It said you were a loving husband and father. And I thought, *That wasn't a very loving thing to do to them.*

That's kind of undeniably true. But it's also a truth with nowhere to go.

Know why I took your death so hard? Two reasons: Because I liked you a lot. And because we were much the same, you and me. And I think we both knew it.

Case in point.

At your memorial, I told a handful of people … no, more than a handful, a big bunch of people … that I loved you, but hadn't really known you. I mean, I recovered with you for years. Sat in that room with you hundreds of times. Both of us telling our truths. Or so I thought.

But it turned out I really only knew you from the outside. From a bit of a distance.

Others said the same was true for them. But that wasn't the airtight proof. This was: when I said the same to your wife. And she pointed to herself. It took me a minute to really fathom what she was saying. That she didn't really know you, either. It's one of those truths you just don't want to fathom. She confirmed it in words, but I don't remember the words exactly.

I just remember a mental image of my own funeral.

Likely there would be hundreds of people there, just like yours. And likely they'd be telling each other how highly they thought of me. Even though they didn't really know me. Only from the outside. Not close up.

Even the ones who were supposed to be closest to me. Who were supposed to know me best. Even the equivalent of my wife, if I had such an equivalent.

At that moment I understood the only really significant difference between you and me now that you were gone: for me it wasn't too late.

Every time somebody talks about you at a meeting, which is often, they always remember the same thing about you. They mention the way you used to always say, "but … it's okay." You'd share some trial that sounded like enough to break somebody's spirit. Then you'd say, "but … it's okay."

To this very day I wonder why we took you at your word.

I don't want to have to say there was a lesson for me in the end of your life, because I don't want to make it sound as though good can come out of a thing like that. Not really. Not in my opinion. The best that can come out of your tragedy is the avoidance of another tragedy. The tragedy you've already carried out is a sealed deal. Future tragedies are optional.

Here are two things I learned from you (though you chose the worst way in the world to teach them to me):

First, I have to let somebody in. All the way in. I don't have to let everybody in. In fact, I don't think we were meant to. But I don't think we were meant to let nobody in, either. I think the truth has to lie somewhere in between.

The second thing, and it's simpler: don't say it's okay unless it is.

Mt. Katahdin

Angels Among Us

For more photos related to this story:
http://www.catherineryanhyde.com/the-long-steep-path/mt-katahdin/

This is a story from back in that bygone era (okay, 2004) when my hiking style was just a tad bit less sane than it is now.

One day I opened my *Backpacker Magazine* and found a picture of the Knife Edge "trail" to the summit of Mt Katahdin. (I have yet to identify the "trail" aspects of this route, even in person, other than blue blazes on the jagged rocks over which I scrambled.)

It was love at first sight.

I was so smitten that I googled more photos of the mountain and sent them to a couple of friends with the message, ATTACHED PLEASE FIND A PHOTO OF MY NEW LOVE, WHICH JUST HAPPENS TO BE A MOUNTAIN. WHETHER THIS WILL MAKE IT MORE OR LESS PAINFUL THAN OLD LOVES REMAINS TO BE SEEN.

Just to give you some idea what we're dealing with here, the mountain itself is a mile high. There are other ways to reach the summit that don't involve the Knife Edge. I guess they were made for sane people.

What's crazy about the Knife Edge?

Nothing much. Really.

Just the fact that it's as narrow as three feet in places.

With drop-offs of several thousand feet.

On each side.

And that it gets very windy up there.

And the weather can change suddenly.

And it's so high up in the clouds that conditions can turn to full whiteout in a heartbeat.

And people do occasionally fall to their deaths.

Other than that, no worries.

It's also in Maine. And I'm in California. So there was a full diagonal continent keeping us apart. Which, as far as I was concerned, is what planes are for.

I booked a flight. I booked a rental car. I booked a few nights at the Big Moose Inn and Cabins in Millinocket. I trained hard.

I flew all the way across the country, landed at Bangor Airport, drove my rental car to Millinocket and settled into a quaint room upstairs (I would later regret the stairs part of the equation) at the Big Moose.

In the morning I drove to the park. Found the trailhead. Scoped out the area. Read the signs that detailed all the many kinds of trouble you might be about to bring down on your head.

I ate and rested most of the day.

I tried to get some sleep.

And yet I found I had … how shall I say … misgivings.

I don't know how much it helps to have hiking buddies in a situation like the one I found myself in that prehike night. I expect buddies may provide moral support. Yet I imagine that after lights-out there are still plenty of misgivings in those individual heads in the dark.

But … the Knife Edge … alone.

I had a fleeting thought. *I need some kind of angel looking after me up there.* But of course it was followed by the more grounded thought. *I would have to be responsible for my own safety.*

I slept some. Not as much as I would have liked.

I arrived in the morning before the gate into Baxter State Park had even been opened. I joined the short line of waiting cars and had a little snack.

A few minutes later I drove in, parked, signed in outside the ranger's station. (I guess so they know who they're looking for in the event that you don't stumble down and sign out again.) Headed up the Helon Taylor Trail to Pamola Point.

Pamola Point is the place where the Helon Taylor Trail ends, and you pick up the Knife Edge. It's also the place where you stop and really assess the weather. It's strongly advised that hikers not go beyond Pamola Point in bad weather.

Bad weather, of course, being a relatively subjective term.

Legend has it that Pamola Point is also the spot at which smart hikers say a prayer to the Mountain Gods. You know. Safe passage and all that.

I knew the Helon Taylor Trail was hard. Because I'd read that many hikers force themselves over the Knife Edge just so they don't have to backtrack down anything as steep as the Helon Taylor.

I'm not sure quite what I expected, based on that assessment. Whatever it was, the mental image was far different from what I encountered that morning.

Here was my most basic misunderstanding, despite rigorous research: I still thought this was going to be

a trail. You know. Based on the fact that they called it
… a trail.

Not so much.

Trails have tread. They might get a bit rocky. But
you more or less walk them. On your feet.

The higher I got, the more I encountered boulders—
of the large variety—that had to be scrambled with
hands and feet, both. I'd never done this type of climbing. I rather hope I never do again.

I made it up to Pamola Point, already feeling that
the "hike" was more than I'd bargained for.

The weather was borderline at best.

The wind was not exactly howling, but it was brisk.
Right on the line, if I were to be completely honest.
A cloud sat on top of the summit. I waited to see if it
planned to lift, or sink down and plunge the mountain
into whiteout conditions.

I wasn't exactly alone at this point. A few other hikers were sitting it out with me. Waiting to see which
way the weather planned to go.

I was joined by two guys. Rob and Paul. They lived
about a state away. New Hampshire, I think they said.
Rob had made it this far twice, but had not yet managed to get the right weather to allow him to proceed.
He was motivated to make it this time. And I'd flown
from the other end of the country. I was motivated to
make it this time, too.

Still … it's not the kind of situation you play around
with.

"Want to go over with us?" Rob asked. "We're going to stick close together and look out for each other.
You know. Safety in numbers."

I thanked him, but said I worried I'd slow them down too much.

As it turned out, they were waiting for a much slower member of their group. A husband and wife hiking pair. The husband was already struggling. So maybe we wouldn't be such a bad speed match after all. But that was all a moot point unless the weather cleared.

We sat and watched it for a time. I had some choices to make.

"Okay," I said suddenly. "If you decide you're going over, I'll go with you."

Half an hour later, the weather hadn't changed *much*. But the small change seemed to be in our favor. The wind was not going to ease up. If anything it would rise. If we were going to go, we knew we had best go ahead and go.

"Let's do it," Rob said.

And we did.

Just as we made our way out onto the Knife Edge (which, counterintuitively, involved some brief elevation loss) Paul looked to his right. I was behind him. When he turned his head, I saw the fear in his eyes.

I felt it deep in my gut, as well. It was contagious. It brought home the reality of our situation. But you can't linger in such a place for long. Literally or figuratively. A moment later it was time to put fear aside and deal with the challenge at hand.

Only later did I learn that Paul is afraid of heights.

The wind was a little too strong. Once I felt as though it was knocking me off balance. Of course, I corrected. Now and then I had to put a knee down, because I just couldn't step up as high as the next foot-hold.

Rob checked in at one point to see how I was doing. I said I was doing just fine. And I was. I was being quiet and withdrawn, but only because I was concentrating completely. I was in the moment, I was being careful, and I was doing it. I didn't know how well I was doing until he asked. The question caused a validating sense of optimism to surge inside me. From a place I had neglected to check.

I got to the summit after Rob and Paul, but before the slower couple. I shouted to them, "I did the Knife Edge! Past tense! And I'm never going to do it again as long as I live!"

We high-fived. Took pictures of each other with the summit sign. It was pretty darned white up there. Still, that photo is one of my favorites to this day.

That was only half of our hike, though. We still had to get down.

We headed across the top of the mountain on some-thing I can only describe as a trail. With packed dirt. I was so excited, and so relieved.

I said, "I recognize this! I know what this is! We have these in California!"

Everybody laughed.

It was a light moment.

I have a photo I took while walking behind Paul on this flat crest of mountain, on our way to connect with the slightly kinder, gentler downhill trail. The hiking was easy. The Knife Edge was behind us. I still remem-ber the lightness of the feeling.

I was happy.

My giddiness was short-lived.

The downhill trail was brutal. If this was the kind one—and it was—God forbid I should ever experience the cruel one.

By the time we made it back within a mile or two of the trailhead, I had taken my poles out of my pack and was using them almost like crutches. Leaning on them to keep my quad muscles from giving out. To keep my legs from going right out from under me on each step. I was slowing down. A lot.

Rob stayed right beside me.

"Go on," I said. "Go down without me. You know I'm going to make it okay from here."

He wouldn't hear of it.

"We started this together," he said. "We're going to finish it together."

We all five exchanged fist bumps and brief hugs in the parking lot, along with email addresses. Then I found my way to my rental car.

I was halfway back to the Big Moose before it hit me.

I got the angel I'd asked for.

This is not to say that I think Rob was any kind of otherworldly being. I'm sure he was not. Undoubtedly he was a regular human guy. But I'd felt like I needed some teamwork, some looking after, and he stepped up and offered some. So that day he was my angel.

We can be angels to each other. We *are* angels to each other, all the time. And we should be. No divine intervention required. Just a sense of staying together and looking out for each other.

You know. Safety in numbers.

Harvey

One Sentence is All It Takes

I knew Harvey from my local community for twelve-step recovery, one of the toughest and most satisfying journeys of all. And it's a journey never taken alone. But twelve-step groups are anonymous. So I'm not just withholding Harvey's last name as a privacy issue. I never knew it. He was just Harvey and I was just Catherine.

Oh. And we were both recovering alcoholics.

An older gentleman, Harvey had a face like an old 1940's movie idol. The more you got to know him, the more you saw his capacity for genuine love. Which is a nice way of saying he didn't wear it on his sleeve. He didn't hand it out to just anybody, for just anything. But when you earned his friendship, you had it. Permanently. It was a solid entity, unlikely to flutter away.

The program is full of people who will love you the minute you walk through the door. One wonderful woman, Barbara—who is still one of my best friends to this day—hugged me right off the bat and told me, "We're going to love you until you can love yourself." And I believed that she did love me, though I couldn't imagine why.

But Harvey … Harvey hung back. He was dignified, discerning. His trust level required building. He didn't rush in with the first hug.

I remember him sharing in a meeting about running into members of the program outside of "the rooms." Around our small town. How odd it felt to him to have become a person who would embrace someone in public. How his old self would have marveled at how much had changed.

Still, Harvey didn't embrace me when he saw me in town. Yet.

Harvey had a heart attack in my second year, and, as he rehabbed his way back from it, I often saw him walking on Moonstone Beach Drive, and we'd walk together.

On one of these walks he asked me how much time I'd accumulated. I told him the exact date on which I'd celebrate two years. I still remember the way he pumped his first in the air, the sparkle in his eyes. It was genuine. He was truly happy for me. I guess by then he knew me well enough to invest his love.

But, those instances aside, Harvey's dramatic influence on my life is almost all contained in one sentence. That is, one sentence of *his*. It will take me longer than that to relate it. But he inspired me—changed the direction of my life, in fact—by speaking one sentence.

I had left my job as tour guide at the Hearst Castle in San Simeon, CA. I had worked as a baker for several years, but then I'd hurt my back. People don't realize that bakers have to be capable of heavy lifting. But they do. After a period of disability, I was in the market for a new line of work.

I just wasn't sure what that should be.

The Friday night meeting had just let out, and Harvey and I were standing on the corner discussing my situation. Coincidentally, it was the corner in front of the first bakery where I had ever worked.

I remember we were under a streetlight, and Harvey was talking about a book called *What Color is Your Parachute?*, a sort of practical manual for job hunters.

Then he looked right into my eyes, and said that one sentence:

"You strike me as the kind of person who could do just about anything you put your mind to."

I knew, even as he said it, that Harvey wouldn't have said a thing like that if he hadn't thought it was true. I had seen with my own eyes that a Harvey compliment was a well-considered opinion. Nothing came flying off the top of his head.

So Harvey really believed that about me. Now the question was, What did *I* believe about me?

I chose to believe that Harvey knew best. That he had seen something in me, and that I could—and should—trust his observation.

In the day or two that followed, I decided that if I could do anything I set my mind to, I would do what I'd always wanted to do. I would be a writer. And, though I had to supplement my income with various part-time jobs for eight years, I've been a writer since that day.

I stepped onto a different path, and I've never stepped off again. All because of Harvey's one sentence.

One sentence might not seem like a lot for a person to do, as inspiration goes. But inspiration is not always commensurate with the time it takes to impart it. That one sentence, from the right person, at the right time, meant more to me than most of the compliments I've received in my life put together.

And maybe that's the key, anyway, the real emotional heart of the thing: to stop assuming that only big contributions on our part can have a big effect on others. To know that a simple sentence, from one person's perspective, could be a complete game-changer to someone else.

Now, part of me was tempted to notice that I'd said encouraging things to other people, and it never changed them much.

But then I had to ask myself, *Really? Are you sure? How do you know?*

I reminded myself that it took me another eight years to break through and publish a book. And make a living at what I'd chosen to do. And by then, Harvey had died. So he probably didn't think he'd ever inspired anyone in one sentence, either.

And, yes, I do know that Harvey's dying before I could tell him this story is a recurring theme in my life, with a strong message. Now I tell people if they've helped me, and I tell them as soon as I can. Because I've learned my lesson. They don't last forever.

Meanwhile, I try to say sentences to others that may change their lives. Even though I can never really know which sentences those might be. But the catch is, I have to mean it. I have to be a person who wouldn't say it if it wasn't true. Because, for it to be truly meaningful, they have to believe me.

And I try not to get too caught up in seeing results, because sometimes we don't get to.

I focus instead on sharing a lot of inspiration, as often as I can. As if I were tossing seeds. Some will blow away in the wind, and some will be neglected, not watered, by their recipients. But the simple law of averages dictates that, sooner or later, a few seeds will take hold.

Harvey's did.

Pat

Slowly, Slowly

Dear Pat,

Here are a few things I carelessly left unsaid.

First of all, I want to thank you for getting my skittish butt into that writers' workshop. Even though it's only in retrospect that I'm able to admit it was fear keeping me away. At the time, sure, I was making cool and reasoned judgments as to whether that was the place for me. You know. If that was the experience that would hone my craft most effectively.

I was ever so discerning in those days.

Did you know I was scared witless?

If so, thank you for keeping that to yourself until I was able to figure stuff like that out on my own.

I also want to thank you for some of the things you said in that Saturday morning twelve-step meeting, where I saw you literally hundreds of times. Some things you said many times, but it works best that way. Recovering people seem to need that kind of repetition. We're anything but quick studies.

A couple in particular I want to thank you for.

Thank you for letting me know I have a knower. Not that you ever told me I did, exactly. But when you told me *you* did, that there were things *you* knew with *your* knower, I checked inside myself.

Imagine my surprise.

That was a good thing for you to leave with us.

If you had to leave us.

Also, that thing you said about how we weren't really trying to kill ourselves. How it must have seemed to others that we were slowly committing suicide, and how even we, looking back, tend to think we must have had a death wish, but ... thank you for saying we weren't trying to kill ourselves. That we were trying to kill the pain.

Every set of lungs in that room breathed the same exhale when you said it. You could hear the unscheduled reaction to the truth of those words as they registered in every heart at once.

Also, thank you for letting me steal that line from you to weave into my first novel. So everyone could think it was me who knew so much about life. Right, two years clean and sober. I was every bit that deep already.

Not.

But, as you also used to say ... and I think I appreciate this most of all ... "slowly, slowly."

We still say that, you know. All the time. In that Saturday meeting. Post-Pat. Someone will always muse about how gradually change comes to them, no matter how hard they work.

Then they'll say, "But ... as Pat used to say ... "

And we all know what comes next before it's even spoken.

I thought about "slowly, slowly" when I was writing some of my hiking stories. Page after page I tried to explain how I learned to give myself more time. To stop timing my ascent. To stop accusing myself of going too slowly. To use stepping stones to achieve goals over a period of months, rather than looking up to the summit and trying to leap from here to there in one fluid bound.

Dozens of pages just to lay out a fancy version of "slowly, slowly." When sometimes the simplest version is the best of all.

Funny how those bits of wisdom came flowing out of your recovery and created the bricks and mortar of mine. I guess that's how we do things in this program. Or this life. You had more sober time, so you stood farther up the path and held a light for people like me.

But by the time we reached you, of course, we hadn't reached you at all. By the time we'd reached the spot where we thought we'd find you, you were farther up still. By then it was impossible to look back at our path and know how much of it was your recovery and how much of it was ours.

As if it mattered.

One more thing I want to thank you for. Those kisses you used to place in the palm of our hand. The way you'd take hold of our hand, open it up flat, plant a kiss in the center of our palm, and fold our hand around it, telling us to put it in our pocket for later.

I never remembered to take them out later. That means I still have a few tucked away somewhere.

Now, having gotten the *thank yous* out of the way, I have a bone to pick with you.

Why didn't you quit smoking before it was too late?

I mean, not at the end there, when I went to see you that last time, and we sat out on the balcony upstairs and looked out at the sea. And you smoked a cigarette. I knew you hadn't quit, and I knew why not. By then it wouldn't have changed anything anyway. Nothing would have.

As disturbing as it was to watch a person smoke and have lung cancer at the same time, I more or less understood.

But what about all those previous years?

Oh, hell, I quit smoking more times than any person I know. Twenty times at least. I know how hard it is as well as anybody.

So I guess it's not so much a why. It's more of a ... damn it.

I know you were anything but a kid. It's not like you were cut off in the prime of your youth. The thing is, we weren't ready to be without you. You took yourself away from us too soon.

Is that what those extra kisses were for? Did you figure we might need some after you were gone?

Well, that's just some bits and pieces of what remains on my mind. Yeah, I think part of me still regrets the way you left. And maybe I'm still a little mad at you for it. But I'll get over it. And I don't think I even need to tell you how.

Deborah

What Rises From Adversity

This is one of those stories that found its roots in tragedy. It's a journey through adversity, both in the moment and in the distant past.

I'm particularly fascinated with that type of travel. Because we all hate tragedy and adversity so much. We'd clear it from our lives in a heartbeat if we could. But then what would happen to the fruit that so often grows from those strange and unwanted seeds?

I guess we'll never know, because there's no way to clear trouble from our lives. I've tried. We've all tried. We're all stuck with some degree of adversity, which I suppose is why I'm tempted to focus more on the fruits.

I'd recently had a problem with an estranged relative that became quite disturbingly public. (And, purely as a side note, for anyone who happened to read about it, it tied me back to the name I was born with.)

I changed my name when I was fairly young, and, as a result, I never hear from the people I knew in childhood. They simply don't have a way to jump the name change and find me.

One day in my trudge through adversity I received a Facebook message from someone not among my list of friends.

It said:

> I am always hesitant to descend (even electronically) into someone's life. Nonetheless, here I go. Aren't you my good childhood friend who shared my love of Pepsi and once convinced me to wash the dishes for a quarter (and then tore a paper towel into quarters and handed one to me)?

Now, I hadn't entirely forgotten being a Pepsiholic as a kid, but lots of people drank the stuff. And the quarter incident brought back no memories. And besides, as I said, I never hear from childhood friends. The name change *always* prevents it. It wasn't done for that reason, but I haven't gone out of my way to repair the rift. Because it was a painful past. I was happy enough to leave it behind.

I was all set to write back and say, No, I'm sorry, I think you must have confused me with someone else.

Until I looked at her name.

She was right. This really was one of my best childhood friends! This was Debbie (I called her that twice in my response, with a promise to stop once I settled down), one of my two best friends for most of my elementary school years! Debbie, who lived around the corner from me on Norwalk Avenue! Who used to have a basset hound named Charlotte who my Siamese cat once chased down the street in front of all the neighbors!

That was the good news.

The bad news was that apparently I really did con her into washing the dishes and then trick her out of the quarter. I have no memory of it, but she does, and

I'm sure it's true. I'm also pretty sure I didn't invent that trick from scratch. I'd probably gotten conned with the same bit myself. Too bad that unfairness was what I'd chosen to pay forward to Deborah.

We've been doing quite a bit of catching up. We've begun to make up for lost time.

We (well, mostly she) remembered the names of almost all the popular kids who tormented us. Deborah told me of a later-life encounter with one of those boys, who turned out to be a nice enough guy. I had always suspected that. I'd often thought maybe these kids were handed the role of oppressor just as I was handed the role of oppressed. That they bullied because the system dictated that someone bully and someone be bullied ... and nobody wanted to be on the losing end. And maybe if I met them later, I'd learn that they either didn't remember torturing us, or remembered with regret. I guess it was a good enough theory.

We remembered Mrs. Powers, a fifth-grade teacher driven into a career-ending emotional breakdown by our class halfway through the year. Like Deborah, I hadn't participated actively in the abuse, but neither had I tried to stop it. So maybe that's a truth worth factoring into my understanding.

"It was like Lord of the Flies," Deborah said, and that was a very apt description. More to the point, it was an observation that made me feel less alone. I hadn't made it up, and I was not exaggerating how bad it had been. I know that now. My memory was corroborated.

We shared the things that frightened us. Amazingly, both of our lists contained the same safety film we were shown at school, but she was scared by the little girl lured into the garage by the bad man. I could not shake the house fire scenes.

We shared the moments that made us feel "less than."

We talked about the dysfunction we lived with daily, partly knowing it was very real, partly wondering why it seemed so invisible to anyone and everyone outside our families.

I shared that there were six lines of a poem, written by a boy in class to embarrass and insult me, that I could still remember at age fifty-five.

Deborah shared a few things that still haunted her, and apparently found solace in the fact that I remembered pieces of that past, too. I could corroborate her reality.

We felt less alone in our old pain.

But this is probably the best thing I learned from Deborah as an adult: she liked me. She was my friend because I was fun, she said.

Sounds basic, but I hadn't known that.

Since there were a handful of us who were not popular, and not wanted as friends by most, I guess I thought my friends were my friends more or less by default. That maybe they hung out with me for lack of better options. I didn't realize someone liked me for me.

For some reason my memories of my young self tended toward the negative. I remembered the times when I wasn't nice enough to my friends. Maybe we all do that. But one of my friends found me, and she remembered when I *was* nice enough.

I sent Deborah a package with a sampling of some of my books, so she could read what I've been up to all these years. And I included one of my personalized note cards.

But I didn't write a note on it. I just taped a quarter to the card.

After all, she fulfilled her end of the bargain. And a deal's a deal.

And, hopefully, over the past forty-some years, I've learned to be a better friend.

Years ago, I wrote a novel which was not published and may never be. In it, my main character said the following about perspective: "Finding one's way through a mental perception is like a photo of a rock. Just a rock. Nothing more. Could be smaller that a fist or bigger than Gibraltar. There's just no way to know. Because there's no way to gain perspective. Unless you wrap a fist around that rock. Or park a car in the shade of it."

For all I'm about to say regarding solitude, the perspective I gained when Deborah stepped into the photo of my rock is something we can only do for one another. Never for ourselves.

Such a small act on the part of an old friend. A couple of hours comparing memories. And yet it was enough to change my perception of the path I traveled to get to where I am now.

But Still Spend Time in Solitude

Joshua Tree

Solitude, Solitude, and Solitude

For more photos related to this story:
http://www.catherineryanhyde.com/the-long-steep-
path/joshua-tree/

During the same difficult present-day journey, I felt the strong desire to, as they say, "get out of Dodge." (I reminded myself of those Southwest Airlines Commercials. "Want to get away?" Um … yup.) I was spending too much time on the Internet by day, and awake in bed at night. I felt that getting in the motor home and driving away would be something akin to taking a psychic shower.

I wanted to go where it was quiet, because even the idea of being surrounded by quiet felt almost like being cleansed.

I made reservations at Indian Cove, at Joshua Tree National Park. And I took my mom, and my dog, Ella, because I knew they could use a psychic shower, too.

But when I went out on the trail—no dogs are allowed on Joshua Tree trails—I was in solitude.

In most cases, when I'm in the outdoors, I'm in solitude.

There's a simple reason for this, and it doesn't involve being wildly antisocial, though I expect I might be, at least from the perspective of some. I just really don't know anyone who likes to hike the way I do. Or, as one friend so tactfully put it, "I like to hike, but you're crazy."

But I also started hiking alone as a way to learn more trust in myself.

I think initially I had an inner sense that I would get in trouble out in the wilderness, and there'd be nobody there to get me out of it. What I wanted was to develop some confidence, to know I could be trusted with my own welfare, and if a problem arose, I could handle it.

I wanted to be the one I trusted to get me out of a jam.

Which is exactly what I accomplished.

We put a lot of confidence in others. Maybe too much, sometimes.

Friends would say, "What if you get lost?"

Well, I reasoned, if there's one of me, there's one of me lost. If there're two of us, there's a very good chance we'd both be lost.

Somehow we assume that we are fallible and others are not. That in a pinch they will handle everything. I wanted to have that same sort of confidence in myself.

That said, I don't kayak alone in the ocean, I don't sleep alone in the wilderness, and I don't hike alone on trails that will likely not see another hiker that day. The one true benefit of a buddy is that they can run tell someone if you are in trouble. But a fellow hiker who is a stranger will do that as well.

I also always leave word at home of exactly where I am and when I expect to return.

Now. Having gotten those disclaimers out of the way ...

I headed out on foot, down Indian Cove Road to the Boy Scout Trail. I didn't hike the entire trail. That would have required a car shuttle, or a night camped out in the wilderness. And besides, I'd read that the trail was sketchy in places and required good route-finding skills. Which makes it less than ideal for the lone hiker. So I vowed to turn back at whatever point I felt I was in danger of being unable to retrace my steps.

I was able to hike the trail to its elevation peak before turning around.

I was out for about four and a half hours before I stumbled back into camp. I did not see one other human being. I did not hear one man-made sound, other than my own footsteps.

While I hiked, I thought about my first trip to Joshua Tree ever. I had chosen to celebrate the Winter Solstice by being outdoors, hiking, for all the daylight hours. From dawn to sundown. It seemed appropriate. Maybe, simply, because it's the shortest day of the year, and the easiest day to make such an odd vow.

I started that long-ago morning walking through an inch or two of snow to Eureka Peak, in the northwest corner of the park. I could tell by the fresh fall of snow that I was the first to have walked the trail that morning. With one exception. For about two miles, the tracks of one lone coyote stretched before me in the snow. But I never saw the coyote. So I guess it still qualifies as solitude.

I've hiked a lot of miles and have been impressed many times by nature, but I always remember those lone coyote tracks, and I always associate them with solitude.

That day, and this one, I had to be sure I was careful in finding my way. This was the kind of solitude that breaks the guidelines I'd set for myself. I had no guarantee that anybody would hike this trail behind me. The only one who could get me home was me.

I had heard, or read, years ago, a theory on why so many people won't carpool or use public transit. Because, for a great number of those people, their daily commute to work and back is the only time they're alone. The only time they can listen to silence, or play their own music, or think thoughts that no one else interrupts.

So here I am, seemingly going in two directions at once. Figuratively, I mean. Not on the trail, but in my praise of humans, and the complete absence of them. I need other people for the perspective they provide. Until I need them to go, so I can think. And then I get my direction on my own, in a place where the only noise—if I stop crunching over gravel—is the wind in my ears.

Except for the kind of direction we can only give each other.

And I won't pretend that my preference at any given time isn't closely tied to how much the people around me are pleasing me, or causing me pain. I'm only human in that regard.

So, which has more effect on my route through the world, through my life? Lifesaving connections with others? Or the time I spend avoiding them, hearing only birds? Wanting to hear only birds?

It's like asking if I prefer day or night. I can't imagine having to give up one for the other.

In a life of balance, I don't believe we're meant to choose one over the other.

Stay in the Moment as Much as You Can

The Wave

You Are Here (Hopefully)

For more photos related to this story:
http://www.catherineryanhyde.com/the-long-steep-
path/the-wave/

If there's one thing I've learned, it's that it hardly matters what path I'm on if I'm not really there. If I'm a million miles away in my head, regretting a past I can't change, or trying to structure or repair a future that hasn't even arrived.

One of my biggest challenges is just to be on the path I'm on.

So, a story about being where I am. Present tense. All systems awake.

It's barely dawn, and my feet are barely planted at the Wire Pass trailhead. I am bizarrely close to the state line of Arizona and Utah—bizarre in that I will hike from one state into another more than once today. I'm in a Bureau of Land Management wilderness called, in varying stages, Paria Canyon, Vermillion Cliffs and Coyote Buttes North.

Like many eager hikers every year (though there would be many more without the stringent permit system) I have come to locate, on foot and in deep sand, a couple of acres of sandstone magic that have been informally dubbed The Wave.

This hike has already given me plenty of lessons in acceptance and staying in the moment. And, as mentioned, so far I'm only standing at the trailhead. It's just before dawn.

But yesterday …

Yesterday I (paradoxically) gave up my dream of this world-class scenic hike. The one I've looked forward to since I miraculously secured a permit on my first try last December.

Yesterday I arrived at the Bureau of Land Management (BLM) contact station to confirm that my little RV would be okay on the dirt road to the Wire Pass trailhead. It's impassible in wet weather. And it's been a wet spring.

The woman took one look at my rig and shook her head. "I wouldn't," she said. Then she pulled out a picture of the steep-banked and amply flowing dirt wash I'd have to drive through. She was right. It was four-wheel drive territory.

The dream flew away. For a moment.

Then she said the beautiful, magic word. "Unless … "

Turns out the trailhead is accessible from the other end of the same horrible dirt road. Just as badly rutted. Twelve miles longer. But no river to cross.

It took me nearly half the day to drive around to reach this trailhead from the other end. Through Page, Arizona. Past the Glen Canyon Dam and Lake Powell. Past Lee's Ferry, on a highway ultimately headed for the North Rim of the Grand Canyon. Then twenty miles up this rutted dirt swath … at an average speed of about ten miles per hour. Sometimes as slow as five.

It took two hours just to navigate the dirt road, carefully steering around, or straddling, ruts deep enough to take out my exhaust pipe or my sewer outlet.

Oh, and did I mention that it was essentially unmarked? That I reached a couple of intersections and could only guess?

But in time I found a sign, then the State Line Campground, which is another term for ... well, nothing. No water, no services, no nothing. But it was the most beautiful nothing I'd ever seen.

A road that can easily disable your vehicle, especially when you're miles from any roadside assistance, will keep you in the moment.

Now it's hike day, and here's another factor that helps keep me present.

When I "won" this permit (there's an online lottery for ten advance permits per day), I was given a brochure with some info on finding the small but magic area called "The Wave" in this endless BLM wilderness. The brochure makes it very clear that it's possible to get lost.

Lost. As in, no one might see you for a long time.

Okay. Got it. So, for a whole twenty-four hours now, I've been paying very careful attention.

I even bought a small entry-level GPS receiver for the trip. My first ever. It points wildly in nearly every direction, and occasionally turns itself off. Know why I never had one before? Because I think they can be dangerous. I think relying on it could cause me to pay less attention, and get more lost. That is, if it lets me down. Which mine seems determined to do.

So I double- and triple-check the visual details. And I arrive at The Wave. And I remember the other way to stay in the moment. It's the best way of all.

Look at something so beautiful, so unusual, so visually arresting that you can't take your eyes off it.

You know the arrow on the directory map that says, You are here?

I am here.

And, in being here, I'm part of something as big as all of nature. And I don't have to think about it, or reach for it. I *am* it.

Before I'd ever hiked the Grand Canyon—which is to say, before I'd ever hiked—three people who had been there told me they felt the presence of God/the Universe/the Powers That Be. There. In the Grand Canyon.

Part of me thought, *Wow. Cool. I want to go.*

Another part of me thought, *How can God be more in the Grand Canyon than anywhere else?*

Now I know.

When I'm in a place like that—or a place like this—I don't go away in my head. It doesn't let me. It doesn't let me wander off to plan what I'll have for lunch (an irritating habit of mine). It rivets me in the moment. This moment.

So, I say to myself, *here's the sixty-four-dollar question: Does divinity live in the Grand Canyon, or The Wave? Or does divinity live in this moment?*

I know the answer, of course. I know I do, and I've always known I did. I just forgot to think about it that way.

Now the trick is to occasionally remember. To stop and ask myself, *What path are you on right now?* To remind myself, *Everything you need is here. It just helps a lot if* you *are.*

My Daily Dog Walk

Look Up and See the Whale

For more photos related to this story:
http://www.catherineryanhyde.com/the-long-steep-
path/daily-dog-walk/

Almost every day, unless I'm traveling, or on a more strenuous hike somewhere else, I walk my dog Ella on the boardwalk at Moonstone Beach, in my little town of Cambria. Now and then I'll run into a local I know. But, since Moonstone Beach Drive is lined with motels and inns, most of my fellow walkers are tourists.

Some walk hand-in-hand, enjoying the view. Which is nice.

Many stop to take photos. Also nice.

And others are on their cell phones, lost in the conversation, eyes trained toward their feet.

This I find perplexing.

I have nothing against cell phones per se. And I completely understand how easy it is to lose track of the moment. I used to be every bit as guilty of doing so, and I still have to constantly remind myself to be where I am. So I bring this up not as a criticism, but as a helpful suggestion.

Maybe it will help someone if I share the questions I ask myself throughout the day. They are as follows:

Where are you now?

Now ... are you really there?

Or is your body there and your mind somewhere else?

I know it's not easy. Success comes seconds at a time, then gets lost again. But what could be more important, more an essential element of life, than remembering to enjoy the beauty of what's right in front of us?

So, to the tourist on your cell phone, here's a partial list of what you missed. What you might have seen if you had hung—and looked—up.

You might have seen waves crashing.

And seals sunning.

A closer look at the rocks might have revealed sea stars and red crabs.

There are almost always surfers surfing.

And often there are otters swimming.

In the spring there are wildflowers growing.

The brown pelicans fly overhead, and sometimes they surf, too.

But, I'm sure your phone call is important. It's just that … I figure you saved up and probably looked forward to this trip for a while. And it just seems a shame to miss it. But if that's not enough reason to hang up, well, that's all I've got.

Oh, wait. One more incentive. Sometimes pods of pilot whales (people mistake them for dolphins because they're small for whales) play very close to shore.

And often a spout or even a fluke can be seen between the shore and the horizon.

But it's up to you to set your own priorities.

Meanwhile at least your phone call is a good reminder to me to hang up whatever thoughts I'm caught up with in my head.

I can think later.

Those of you who read *The Day I Killed James* may remember the line about looking up and seeing the whale.

It started when Theresa was riding up the Big Sur Coast on the back of James's motorcycle. And he sticks his arm straight out, cliff side, pointing at something. But Theresa "realized too late it was a pointing thing." She never saw what he saw.

Later, when they stopped for coffee at Ragged Point, she asked him.

"What were you pointing at back there?"

He said it was a whale. Breaching.

But Theresa had been so preoccupied thinking about her boyfriend and his new girlfriend, she'd forgotten to notice there was even an ocean out there.

Later, after James has driven his motorcycle and himself off a cliff, Theresa is finally able to see what she had in him.

"Know what it was like?" she asked. "It was like I finally looked up and saw the whale."

The unfortunate truth is that it's often the loss of someone or something important that helps us break through to a clear knowledge of its value. But, of course, by design, it's then too late.

So this little collection of thoughts is a reminder, to myself and others, to look up and see the whale.

Speed

Why is Everybody in Such a Hurry?

I'm about to admit something about myself that only my close friends know. It has not been public knowledge until now. It's probably going to put a lot of you off and make you really mad at me. Some of you might not even like me any more. You may slam this book shut in disgust.

But no more hiding. I'm getting this off my chest.

I drive the speed limit.

And it drives (no pun intended) my fellow motorists out of their minds.

Now, I'd like to note, in my own defense, I don't drive *slower* than the speed limit. I just don't drive *faster*.

I don't mean for it to make everybody nuts. It's not my goal to slow anybody down. But I live on a two-lane highway. If I'm doing the speed limit, the guy behind me has to do the speed limit as well. If I could let him by, I would. If there's a turnout, I turn out.

I used to pull over onto the right shoulder. Across the white line. But it turns out that's the bike lane, so that's blatantly illegal. So now I don't.

So other drivers, for the most part, drive right up my tailpipe. Half the time I can't even see the headlights of the car behind me, it's so close. Does the driver think he can bully me into going faster? If so, he's wrong. He's just putting us both in jeopardy.

I realize this is a bit of a delicate topic, because the driver whose headlights I can't see may very well be you.

So, just for the sake of this little gathering of thoughts, can we lay down our differences and speak without judgment?

What seems a little off-kilter to me is that I don't judge people for breaking traffic laws. They're more than welcome to, if they're willing to pay the citation. And as far as an accident being more likely—which it is at higher speeds, let's face statistics—I can just direct my energy into trying to be somewhere else when it happens. But if their behavior is any indication, most drivers judge me harshly and unmercifully for *not* breaking the law. And that seems odd.

Here's what I'd like to say to you, if we weren't careening down a two-lane highway at fifty-five miles per hour.

First of all, I used to be just like you are now. I pressured people to speed up. I passed on double yellow lines. I took hairpin curves at twice the posted speed. So I know how it feels.

I also know there's no reason for it.

You have no idea how sticky this feels to me, because I only know maybe one other person who drives the speed limit. Every friend I have is on the other side of the speed limit spectrum from me. I've heard every comment there is to be made about it. Trust me. There's no reason for it.

Well, there are two stated reasons, but they both fall down when you shine the light on them.

One: "I'm in a hurry to get where I'm going. I don't want to be late."

Me, neither. I hate being late. So I leave the house five minutes earlier than you do. Problem solved.

Two: "It drives me out of my mind when people go too slow."

Yeah, I get that. I not only get it, but I remember it. Clearly. But that's a feeling. It's not a reason. Nobody ever says, "Gosh, it just drives me crazy not to rob banks, so that's why I rob them."

If we can really be honest with each other for a minute, it's a compulsion. Take it from one who was formerly compelled. We're all running around in a frantic hurry, and we don't know why.

Years ago, when I was only seventeen, living on my own in New York City, the speed of the city began to get under my skin. When I first got there, I wouldn't have been caught dead crossing against the light unless it was the middle of the night with no cars as far as the eye could see. In less than a year, I woke up in the middle of an intersection (figuratively speaking) and realized I had joined a crowd of pedestrians in stepping off the curb and literally stopping oncoming traffic. Here's the kicker: it was my day off. I was on the way to the park. You know. Just to kill some time.

I left New York immediately.

But I still drove too fast. Way too fast. As fast as I thought I could get away with driving. Bizarrely, and as a result of nothing but blind luck, I never got a speeding ticket.

I slowed down considerably when I became a starving author. My resources were so scant, I just couldn't see wasting that kind of money on traffic fines and increased insurance rates. I slowed *almost* all the way down. To within two to five miles of the limit.

Usually.

Then something interesting happened to change everything. I got a red car. And, because red cars get more speeding tickets, I decided slowing down by two more miles per hour wouldn't hurt me a bit.

Everybody I know—and I do mean everybody— said the same thing.

"Oh, you're going to get more speeding tickets now."

"Well, I've never even gotten one, and besides … "

"Oh, well you will now."

"Well, no I won't, because … "

"You will. It's a statistical fact. Red cars get more tickets. Look it up."

I couldn't even get through the sentence on why I wouldn't. They just knew I would. Because it never, for one instant, occurred to them that maybe I wasn't going to speed. Because everybody speeds. Right?

Well. Almost. Everybody minus me. And it's damned uncomfortable.

I have dear friends with thirty and forty years in recovery who have no qualms about telling me, "Oh I have to go fast. I just can't stand going slow. I hate getting behind people like you. I just want to drive right through them."

But they don't know why.

Everybody is racing around breaking the law to hurtle down the road faster, and nobody really knows why. They just know this gut feeling wants them to do it. And that it's really, really uncomfortable if they don't give that feeling what it wants.

But nobody's interested in knowing why.

I don't know why I did, either. Not really. I know that the more I meditate, the less I rush. I know if I stay in the present moment, I can admire the view (okay, I admit it, I live in a pretty place, which gives me some advantage) and feel satisfied being half the way—instead of all the way—to my destination.

But I don't know why that feeling was telling me to rush. I just know it felt awful, and I don't want to be caught up in it anymore.

So, here's what I propose. Can we all just get along?

I know recovering and practicing alcoholics don't tend to get on well together. Can recovering speeders and practicing speeders make peace? I won't drive any faster for you, but I'll pull over where it's safe. And I'm not criticizing you for wanting to go fast. I'm really happy for you to do whatever you think is best, so long as you're not doing it less than a foot behind my rear bumper.

But someday, when it's your day off, and you're on your way to someplace recreational to kill some time, maybe you'll think of this little essay and experiment with the posted speed.

It feels weird at first. Very weird. But you get used to it. Just like any other change. And then it takes on a whole new life and it feels really good. Almost like … relaxing into the world. Knowing you're not late for anything. It's like taking a deep breath.

Try it sometime. You might be surprised. And if you don't like it after a period of adjustment, well … isn't that a turnout up ahead? I'll just pull over and get out of your way.

Valencia Peak

Fogbows and Brocken Spectres

For more photos related to this story:
http://www.catherineryanhyde.com/the-long-steep-
path/valencia-peak/

I've lived in the same small town for more than a quarter of a century, most of that time in the same house. I had two dogs to walk for most of those years, mine and my mom's (or, if she took a walk, she took them both).

A surprising number of those days, I walked the same path through the same woods.

In time, I ceased to see the woods. In fact, I often ceased to notice that I was outdoors at all. I'd go off in my head, which would begin to spin around and around and around. After all, what was there to see? I had already seen it all.

The dogs, I couldn't help noticing, took a different tack. I could tell. They never got bored. They never walked along with their gaze far away, as if they were somewhere else in their heads. They always kept their nose to the wind and followed every sight, sound, and scent.

I began to focus on the difference between the way I dealt with the repetition and the way they approached it. Not surprisingly, it came down to the most basic difference possible between personhood and doghood.

I came to feel that I knew more or less what the dogs would tell me, if they could talk. If we could engage each other in that sort of conversation.

"Gosh," I might say. "It's just this same old path through this same old woods. Don't you get bored?"

"Same?" they might reply. "Same? How can you say it's the same? Don't you smell that tinge of smoke in the air? Someone's burning something a few miles from here. Don't you hear that faint clopping of hooves and crunch of brush? A deer heard us and is running away. And right here—yes, here—a fox came across the trail this morning. And look, I just flushed a few quail out of the brush. That didn't happen yesterday!"

It's taken a long time, but I've learned to be just a little bit more like a dog. Don't knock it until you've taken it for a test drive.

Here's where Valencia Peak comes in.

When I'm training for a big hike, I often return over and over to Valencia Peak in Montana de Oro State Park. There's a simple reason why. In the summer, it's cool. It's one of the rare places near my home where a peak suddenly rises up more than 1,300 feet above sea level, but without taking the hiker more than two miles from the coastline, and without any topography to block the ocean breeze. So on a day that might see a ninety-degree temperature at my second-favorite peak, Cerro Alto, it might only be in the low seventies on top of Valencia.

As a result, I've done that same hike many, many times. More times that I can count.

At first, I'm sorry to report, I did not repeat this hike the way my dog would. I just pitched forward and pounded the trail to the top. I didn't look around much, because whatever was there to see I had already seen.

Or so I thought.

I did learn something interesting from that repetition, though. I learned that my abilities are not the same every day. Before the lesson in question, if I found myself straining on a grade, I assumed the trail was—in some indefinable way—tougher than the distance and elevation would indicate. But after repeated trips up Valencia Peak, I had to concede that the trail was not changing. The only changeable factor was me.

Years ago I had a horse. His name was Cody, and he was only two when I bought him. Still too young to ride. So I gentled him (I did not break him—at the end of the training he was fully intact). I had three minor mishaps in the course of the training. Three spills that hurt. And I summed them up and reported them to the horse trainer who was helping us both.

In all three cases, I had made very good progress the previous day. A breakthrough of some sort. And it caused me to suddenly overschedule the future. *Well,* I thought, *if we can do X today, surely we can do XY tomorrow.* The following day I would hit the rail head first, because I'd failed to notice that the horse was simply not in the same place, not in as good a mood, or not as receptive to my lessons. Or, in the case of this stubborn boy, all of the above.

Turned out our trainer thought that was a good observation.

In my early repetition of Valencia Peak, I learned that the same applies to me as well.

I began rating myself (a tool, not a judgment) on my energy and abilities for that day—on a scale of one to ten. One day I was a nine point five. Next time out a four. No specific trackable explanation, except that I'm flesh and blood, like a horse or a dog. I'm not a machine. I'm more complex.

It's a valuable thing to know. It releases me from some unrealistic expectations I might have of myself.

Then came a time when I didn't hike Valencia Peak for a couple years.

When I got back to doing it regularly, I'm pleased to say, I found myself hiking that little mountain more the way a dog would.

The same? How can you say it's the same? Today I saw a coyote stop and stare at me, put his head down, then race off. Today I got four steps from one of the wild brown bunnies before it hopped to cover. Today I got a glimpse of a bobcat, walking away into the brush.

The more I started watching, the more I saw things I literally did not know existed in the world.

Literally. Did not know existed.

Ever seen a fogbow? It's like a rainbow, but less colorful. And it's not seen on a rainy day. It's a bright arc of whitish light touching the mountain at the edge of the fog. I even got a photo. I posted the photo on my social networking sites, with the message, "Is there such a thing as a fogbow? And, if not, what the heck is this?" No one seemed familiar.

Then, on the very next trip up Valencia, I saw—and photographed—another fogbow.

Here I have to stop and ask questions I can't even answer myself. Would I have seen fogbows all along if I had known they existed? Was it simply a matter of keeping an eye out for them? Remembering to look?

I may never know.

I do know this. When I posted the second fogbow photo, I took a moment to google the word. Frankly, I thought I was being tongue-in-cheek by making it up, but I not only got hits for the word fogbow, I learned there's a Wikipedia page devoted to fogbows.

I posted my new photo on Facebook, along with the link to the Wikipedia page. My friend Shannon, who I had met years before when we were Hearst Castle tour guides together, told me she thought it was called a *Spectre of the Brocken.*

Okay. More new things to learn.

I googled *Spectre of the Brocken.* Turns out it's that rare phenomenon—apparently involving fog, light, and elevation—that surrounds a shadow with a small, tight rainbow. Apparently, it was first documented on Brocken Peak in Germany.

I had actually seen this phenomenon, once. Years before, when I was flying in a commercial airplane, I looked down and watched the shadow of our plane on the clouds far below, surrounded by this small rainbow. I had no idea what it was, or what to call it. But I had seen the Brocken Spectre.

I still did not think, however, that my fogbows were Brocken Spectres. If for no other reason than their tendency to be bigger and more colorless.

I really am heading somewhere with all of this. Thank you for your patience.

A couple of weeks later, I trudged up Valencia Peak again in the fog. And yes, believe it or not, witnessed my third fogbow. Three hikes out of three. Then I turned around at the apex of a switchback, just as the sun crested the hill behind me, and saw my own shadow on the fog below. Surrounded by a small, tight rainbow.

At first I almost couldn't believe what I was seeing. Was that really me in the center? I raised my arms, waved them around. The shadow in the center waved back at me. I was witnessing the Spectre of the Brocken, not two weeks after learning such a thing existed.

Better yet, I had my camera.

So ... the same? How can you say it's the same? Today I saw my shadow on the fog surrounded by the Brocken Spectre.

I can't really answer questions of coincidence and timing. But I may see less coincidence in the story than some. I think the bottom line here is that the more we see, the more we see. Part of it may simply involve looking up. Part of it may have to do with seeing what we're open to see. I don't know.

I do know that my first spiritual teacher once taught me the classic Zen precept, "You can never step twice into the same stream."

My dogs understood the concept all along. I eventually caught up.

Accept What Is

Pike's Peak Cog Railway

The Bucket List

For more photos related to this story:
http://www.catherineryanhyde.com/the-long-steep-
path/pikes-peak-cog-railway/

As I write this, my mom is eighty-nine years old. She'll turn ninety this spring.

She is in remarkably good health. Astonishingly good health. And fitness. And attitude. And energy. It's really quite easy to forget her age. But sometimes it's better, I think, to take both factors into account.

When she was eighty-three, I took her on a hike down to Cedar Ridge, which is a three-mile round trip into the Grand Canyon, with almost 1,200 feet of elevation gain on the way out. I didn't do this thoughtlessly, or without planning.

Several months earlier, she had taken a fall. Broken her wrist.

It happened just a couple of weeks before she'd planned to take an Elder Hostel trip to the Grand Canyon, which she had never seen. I know how much it hurts to give up a dream like that. So I said, "We'll go to the Grand Canyon in the Spring. I'll take you."

This was before the years of my motor home. It didn't matter. We booked a room at the Maswik Lodge. We would go by car.

When she was properly healed and rehabbed, I began to take her out on the hiking trail with me. And we started to train.

There was a method to my madness.

After an older person falls and breaks a bone, it can be the beginning of the end for them. Well-meaning adult children tell their parents, "Mom. Sit down. Let me do that. You don't want to hurt yourself again." And so the descent begins. And compounds.

I knew this was a moment of truth.

Also, I'd noticed that almost every time she took a fall, it involved a flash of distraction, or a feeling that she had to hurry for someone or something.

So we bought her a pair of hiking boots and poles.

And I slowed down (I'm pretty slow anyway—I call myself a tortoise hiker) and walked right behind her.

And I taught her to put her total attention into her footing.

I taught her to keep a sort of mantra of sure-footed confidence in her head.

I had her practice never looking at the view as she hiked, but rather stopping, looking at the view, then going back to moving her feet and looking where she was going.

By the time she got down to Cedar Ridge, I knew she could do that much distance and elevation. I'd seen it with my own eyes.

The hike up really stretched her to the limit of her capabilities. But then, the Canyon stretches everybody.

Later she told me, glad as she was to have done that, she knew when she got up to the rim that it was the last time she would hike at that level. And I think that's about right.

In the same year, I had a chance to take two free back-to-back cruises on the Mediterranean and Aegean Seas in return for being a cruise speaker. And double occupancy of the cabin didn't raise the price. So I took my mom to Europe. She was eighty-three, and had never had a passport before.

We saw Italy. And Greece. And Tunisia. And France. And Croatia. And we were supposed to see Spain, but a fishermen's strike closed the port at Barcelona. And we never got there.

While in Europe, we decided the following year we'd take a trip to Paris and Barcelona. But by the time we got home, she knew she was done with the rigors of such far-flung travel.

Now, with all this talk of Paris, you probably think I'm rolling in money. But I'm not. That "free" trip ended up costing a fortune in airfare and day tours. It put me in some debt and took a while to pay off. But it didn't matter. Because we just got in under the wire for her. Much later, she wouldn't have been able to enjoy it to the same extent. If she'd have been able to go at all.

People don't lie on their deathbed and think, I wish I hadn't gotten into that debt in 2005 and had to pay my taxes in installments. Penalties and interest are not what we regret. We regret things like, Why didn't I take my mom to Europe while there was still time?

Priorities.

This past September, we traveled to Pike's Peak, so she could ride the Cog Railway to the summit. It's been a sort of bucket list item of hers. Her friend Catherine (no relation to yours truly), since deceased, had done it. And spoken quite highly of it. And it was something my mom really wanted to do.

About two weeks before we were to leave on this trip, things got a bit tight financially ... and, more to the point, her back came up sore.

She made a couple of visits to our local chiropractor. And, with his marginal blessing, she decided to go.

We loaned ourselves enough money for gas and headed out. Sure, it was stretching it. It was not ideal. But if we missed September, we would more or less have missed autumn. I had no intention of driving through the high passes of the Colorado mountains after the snows arrived. Or even after they *could* arrive, if they suddenly chose to. And we couldn't go in spring, because in late spring we have an even bigger and more important bucket-list item. I've promised to take her to Yellowstone for her ninetieth birthday. And we wouldn't go in summer because the kids are out of school, and it's a madhouse out there. So a delay would mean a one-year delay.

I didn't say the dream might not hold a year. She didn't say it. The chiropractor didn't say it. But we must all have known. Because we went to Pike's Peak to ride the Cog Railway to the summit.

I had some concern about the altitude, which is over 14,000 feet. Would she be able to breathe up there?

She did okay. I gave her my arm coming off the train. The way people do when their parents are ... you know ... elderly. Just under the circumstances. It was fifteen degrees on the summit, with a high, stiff wind. So she sat in the restaurant while I walked around outside and took photos.

When I saw the big stone-based sign SUMMIT PIKE'S PEAK 14,110 FEET framed against a brilliant blue sky, I went back inside to get her. She just had to get a picture taken with that sign. And we made it out there. And I got the picture. If you know my mom, it's up on her Facebook page, along with a very flattering photo of her smiling beside the long red train.

By the time we got home, her back was pretty bad, and it was hard for her to move around much. But she took care of herself. And she came around. And I don't think either one of us regretted crossing that important item off the bucket list.

There's only one big deal left on that list. Yellowstone next May.

Wish us luck.

I have a bucket list, too. For a while there, I didn't. I felt I'd done it all. I'd been to India. I'd been to Australia and New Zealand. I'd taken those amazing cruises. I'd visited the White House by invitation. I'd made the bestseller list. I'd backpacked the Inca Trail to Machu Picchu. I'd had my picture in *TIME* magazine.

Really. What's left?

Unfortunately, I've been spending too much time poking around on the Internet. Seeing all the things I've missed. Now I have a whole new list. I should probably call it Bucket List #2.

I want to meet an Atlantic puffin face to face.

I want to trek in Nepal or Tibet, in the foothills of the Himalayas. Because I want to see Everest and Annapurna with my own eyes. I don't want to climb them. I couldn't, and I'd be a fool to try. But I want to see the powdery snow blowing like smoke off their peaks.

I want to lie in bed in one of those glass hotel rooms in Norway and watch the aurora borealis as I drift off to sleep.

I'm not nearly ninety. But then, none of us comes with a longlife guarantee.

So the point of this essay is this: It boils down to a piece of advice.

I'm usually a bit standoffish about giving advice. I subscribe to the theory that one should only give advice when asked, or in a life-or-death situation. But maybe this marginally qualifies as life-or-death. If you don't follow it, it won't kill you. But, looking back at the end of things, you might feel it lowered the quality of the life you led. And we all just have one life, so far as we know and are guaranteed. And we want to use it well.

So here's the unsolicited advice, and thanks for the latitude:

If you have a bucket list, get on it. And if you don't, get on *that*. Get one. And then, get on it. Nobody lives forever.

Notes From a Bad Day

How to Be Happy

A couple of months ago I bought a new pair of Ray-Bans to replace an old scratched-up pair I'd had for years (I get terrible eyestrain headaches from less expensive sunglasses). Yesterday, at a friend's memorial, they were in the pocket of my raincoat when I leaned on and broke them.

Of course, the friend's memorial factors into the bad-day-ness of all this in a much bigger and more concrete way. The Ray-Bans were just a minor add-on, like bad icing on a bad cake.

I thought maybe the sunglasses could be repaired. God knows death cannot.

I wasted some time trying. I didn't succeed in fixing them, but I did poke a nice hole in my finger with the tiny screwdriver in the process.

Then this morning got off to a rocky start. They're building a house behind mine, in what was once a pristine field with an ocean view. And I mean right behind. A few feet from my back fence. They whacked down two beautiful, huge, healthy trees to do it. And now I get to listen to construction all day long.

But that's just one of those things you have to accept. Short of buying the acre lot myself (I tried, but it was beyond me financially), there's nothing much more to be done.

This morning, however, they woke me up at 6:30 A.M. They were out there in the dark, flooding the work area with the headlights of a pickup truck and hammering on something.

I put on my robe, and discussed with them the laws that limit them to a 7:00 A.M. start time.

They expressed contrition (always to be taken with a grain of salt in reference to a purely voluntary act) but that didn't stop the deafening concrete truck from showing up (in reverse—*beep, beep, beep*) at 6:50 A.M.

So let's just say the morning required a little … re-framing.

I had one more conversation with the building foreman, who assured me that this was the last "concrete morning" and the last time they'd be pushing to stay on schedule.

Then I gave up and ordered a new pair of sunglasses.

Later in the morning I was driving through town with Ella (my dog), and surprised myself (and probably her as well) by announcing that I had decided to be happy.

Since that's probably a confusing jump, here are some of my thoughts about happiness: I've been experimenting with the idea that it's a decision.

Now, that's an easy statement to argue. You may say, "But there's so much I can't control, and it makes me unhappy." Right. True. There's a lot we can't control. But if we could be happy anyway, then we could be happy. Case in point: I'm tempted to be unhappy about a house behind my back fence. But there's a house on either side of me, and one right across the street. I look out and see them all the time. And they never make me unhappy.

I've been noticing lately how often we feel we have justified resentments. I hear people say, "I have a right to be upset about this." And I think, *Yeah. Sure you do. But why would you want to be?*

I always have a right to unhappiness, but it's not a right I'm all that anxious to exercise.

I'm having this day, and writing about this day, very shortly before the end of December. So, here's my wish for the New Year: I wish for us to all be happy. And by that I don't mean I wish for every inch of the Universe to line up to suit our preferences. Not because I don't want that for you, or for myself, but because it's—let's face it—not bloody well likely. So my wish is that, whatever comes our way in the New Year, we choose to be happy. Happy with it, happy in spite of it ... it really doesn't matter. I just hope we can choose to be happy.

Wild Indian Monkeys

Walk Softly, But ...

For more photos related to this story:
http://www.catherineryanhyde.com/the-long-steep-
path/wild-indian-monkeys/

When I take my little fifteen-pound dog, Ella, for a walk, I always carry a big stick.

It's taller than my shoulder, made of solid oak. A good inch or more in diameter. It has a rubber cane tip on the bottom, and a leather thong to slip around my wrist. So it's … you know … a real walking stick. Lots of people use them. It has nothing to do with hitting anything.

Probably.

But if I'm going somewhere without her, I don't carry the stick. So I have to admit that its purpose involves her defense.

It all started like this:

Sometime around 2008, I was walking across a piece of what Cambrians call The Ranch. It's formally called the Fiscalini Ranch Preserve, and it's a massive 400 plus acre open space preserve that we were fortunate (and hard-working) enough to be able to buy, thus saving it from otherwise inevitable development. Could have been a sea of condos, but instead it's a series of walking paths. We are blessed to have it.

Only the most popular Ranch trail asks you to keep your dog on a leash. This was one of the less popular ones.

I had let Ella off leash briefly to run around and enjoy the freedom. I was walking along, not noticing that she was catching up with me more and more. Staying closer and closer to my heel.

Finally she made a move I can only describe as the doggie equivalent of pointing nervously over her shoulder. She scooted forward half a dozen running steps, while glancing behind her. She did this within my field of vision. Which, frankly, I think was no accident. She's a smart dog, and it think it was her way of communicating a concern to me.

If I hadn't seen it happen, there might not be an Ella right now.

I saw a movement out of the corner of my eye, which I took to be somebody else's off-leash dog catching up with us.

I turned to look, and found myself staring into the eyes of a wild coyote. (Which I think ... hope ... is redundant. I certainly hope nobody tries to keep one as a pet.) He was very close behind us. Just a big handful of feet. He had been tracking us. Well, tracking Ella.

She had noticed and I had not.

I got hold of her and got her up under my jacket. She listens to me in a pinch when I tell her to hold still, which was a lifesaver in this case.

Then I shouted at the coyote to move off.

Usually that would do it. They're spooky animals, and they don't like to mess with humans, because we're bigger than they are. Still, in the back of my head, I remembered a ranger at Death Valley National Park telling me that, in some areas, in some limited instances, coyotes had been known to attack people for their pets.

Even so, it was Ella I was scared for. Not me.

The coyote did not move off.

Instead, he (yes, I'm making assumptions here) sat down, tipped his head back, and barked. Or, anyway, whatever you call that sound coyotes make.

Another coyote stepped out from behind a stand of brush, and took up a position on the other side of the trail.

They had been flanking us.

If I had walked past that stand of brush, the second coyote would have stepped out and separated off Ella, making it impossible for her to get back to me. And that would have been the end of poor little Ella.

I'm sorry to say these were not properly spooky coyotes. In fact, this newcomer took several steps in our direction. And I wasn't just standing there acting frightened, either. I was shouting at them with every ounce of authority and sheer volume I possess. I was threatening their lives.

But this second coyote still came in our direction.

What I needed at that moment was a big stick. Unfortunately, at the time, I had never thought to carry one.

It was essentially a bluff on the coyote's part. A fake out. Just to see if I'd cave. After a few steps, the creature made a sharp turn and sat next to his friend, looking plenty miffed that I had an issue with something as simple giving up my dog.

They followed us all the way to the highway. Every time I turned around and confronted them with my voice, they'd stop and sit. Every time I turned to walk again, they'd follow.

As Ella and I stepped over the stile in the fence and crossed the highway, I looked over my shoulder to see that they'd finally given up and moved off.

That's when I began keeping Ella on leash at all times, unless we're home or at the dog park. (When your person walks you two to five miles on an average day, that's not as restrictive as it sounds.) It's also when I bought the walking stick.

I'd like to go on record as saying that I don't expect to ever bash a coyote on the skull with the walking stick.

First of all, I may never see one that close again. It's an unusual incident. This happened during the third or fourth year of a drought, and the animals were getting pretty desperate. The mountain lion rules in these parts (or just about any parts where they are present), so coyotes have to take the prey that's left over.

I understand that everybody needs to eat. But I draw the line at my dog.

If I do ever have a close encounter with one again, I still don't expect to bash him over the head with the stick. For a simple reason. Just *having* the stick is likely going to be protection enough. The stick is an interspecies language. It clearly states, If you're smart, you'll go pick on someone who doesn't carry a large, rudimentary weapon.

Having the stick generally precludes *using* the stick.

Now for the part about where I learned this in the first place. The part about the wild Indian monkeys.

I visited India in 2005. I'd been invited there to meet a very old and well-respected swami who, I'd recently learned, was a huge fan of my book *Pay It Forward*, and my Pay It Forward Foundation.

A lovely, funny, and kind young monk named Swami Yatidharmananda had invited me to come to the ashram to visit His Holiness. He even volunteered to come to Delhi to meet my plane. From there we would take the train to Haridwar, then go by hired car to Rishikesh, a village in the foothills of the Himalayas, on the banks of the sacred Ganges River. And I would stay as a guest at the Sivananda Ashram for a couple of weeks.

I corresponded with Yatidharmananda a great deal in preparation for the trip. I also read up on India extensively.

I picked up quite a few warnings.

I was warned that the roads were "congested."

Having lived in LA for twelve years, this didn't sound like much of a threat.

Turned out it was not so much the number of vehicles but their unique style of driving that tourists tended to find so terrifying. The way twenty or thirty head-on collisions are missed by mere inches for every mile or so of travel. But, whatever. I'm a brave soul. I can deal with that. Just as long as they continue to miss.

I was warned that sanitation is not what I would expect it to be. Okay. I got my recommended shots, and my doctor sent me overseas armed with a prescription bottle of Cipro (a wide-spectrum antibiotic) just in case.

I felt prepared. As if I knew a great deal about what I might encounter there.

When Yati and I stepped out of the train station in Haridwar, I looked up at the blue roof of a little shop across the road.

I said, "Monkeys."

There were three wild monkeys sitting on the roof.

"Yes," he said. "Monkeys." As if it was a bit odd that I felt such an obvious fact needed to be stated out loud.

"You have wild monkeys in India."

"Oh, yes," he said.

Now, I'm not inordinately afraid of wild monkeys. I was rather fascinated, in fact. And I truly enjoyed the photo ops they provided. I had no irrational fear of wild monkeys, any more than I have an irrational fear of coyotes. But if two of them decide they want my dog, fear becomes a rational response.

I just thought it was a bit odd that I was warned there would be road congestion, but not wild monkeys. I just questioned those priorities. A bit.

Over the first few days of my stay, I learned that there are a number of rational reasons to be cautious about wild monkeys. For example, if you are bitten by a monkey, the series of necessary shots can be horrendous. Plus, they have been known to form little "street gangs," for lack of a better term, to rob shops and mug tourists. Not just for fun, of course. For food. Um … usually for food. Sometimes the lines blur. But rest assured that if you are carrying food down the street of Sivanandanagar (the district outside Rishikesh where Sivananda Ashram is located), you are a target for a possible … well, perhaps likely … monkey mugging.

They also like shiny objects, and will sometimes take a purse or shoulder bag out of curiosity as to what it might contain.

A few days before I arrived, a monkey took a leather bag off the shoulder of a man walking across the suspension bridge. When he tried to get it back, the thief tossed it back and forth with a few of his friends in a game of keep-away. Finally one of the monkeys carried the bag up onto the cables of the bridge and tossed it into the Ganges River.

But that incident ultimately fell into the category of dratted inconvenience.

A few months prior, an old monk had died from shock and from his injuries after a vicious monkey attack. The old monk had seen a baby monkey lying in the road, hit by a passing vehicle. In a moment of unguarded compassion, he went to the fallen baby and cradled it in his arms. And the mother monkey unleashed all of her protective maternal rage on him.

By now I guess you get the idea. Having begun my trip with no special irrational fear of wild monkeys, I learned the rationality of not becoming victim to any of their thefts, rages, muggings or pranks.

I noticed that some of the many craft stalls sold carved walking sticks. When I inquired as to how many rupees a stick would cost, I was given a price equivalent to about 1.75 US dollars.

So, that's a no-brainer, right?

Depends. In an ashram full of highly spiritual people (and dozens of DO NOT FEED THE MONKEYS signs), I found there were different schools of thought on avoiding simian conflict. Not everyone liked the idea of a stick.

Yatidharmananda advised me. "Think peaceful thoughts toward the monkeys."

So I took his advice, and that's exactly what I did. I bought one of the carved walking sticks, and, as I walked through town with my big stick, I thought peaceful thoughts toward the monkeys.

Needless to say, I was not the victim of any assaults.

Before you think this is a simple tongue-in-cheek story about reserving the option to use force, I'd like to share something I learned years ago in an amazing and comprehensive women's self-defense course called Model Mugging. The course doesn't just teach you where and how to strike an attacker, if you're unlucky enough to have one. It teaches you how not to be unlucky enough to have one.

Here's the first thing I learned in Model Mugging:

A study was done, years ago, using violent predators in our prison system. These men were shown films of women walking down the street. They were asked to choose their victim, just the way they would if they were still out in the streets committing crimes.

They all chose the same women. They all knew their victims the moment they saw them. They reacted to the quickened step, the nervous glance across the shoulder. These are victim moves. These are the tells of fear and vulnerability.

This is does not mean the victim is blamed in any way. Blame is not the point here. Learning how not to be victimized is the point.

The remarkable aspect of the Model Mugging program, in my mind at least, is not just that graduates almost always fend off their assailants if attacked—although they absolutely do—it's that very few graduates are attacked. Compare the statistics to the female population at large, and the message is hard to deny. When you know you can take care of yourself in the event of trouble, you relax and move through the world with confidence. That confidence takes you out of the victim category. And trouble is less likely to find you.

I didn't carry a stick so I could hit a monkey. I carried a stick to assure myself that I wouldn't have occasion to need to.

Before I left, I gave the stick to a new friend, another ashram guest from the U.S., who was finding herself easily cowed by domineering monkeys. Then I flew home, so I have no idea if it helped or not. I hope so.

Now, all three of these stories—the coyote incident, the trip to India, and my Model Mugging course—are many years old. So here's why all this came up to be written today.

A woman I sponsor (a sort of one-on-one advisory relationship) in the program has a dangerous infection, and, though she has sought medical care for it, she is sometimes hesitant to give the illness all the care it needs. When she needed to go back to the hospital, she mightily resisted. She was just sure that in the morning it would be better. Even though there had been no intervention, no additional medical assistance, no medication change to bring about the improvement. But she had adopted what she considered a positive attitude. She was holding a good thought: it would be so much better by morning that no medical intervention would be required.

She said, "Positive thinking is good, right?"

I said, "Yes. Positive thinking is excellent. Now get your butt to the hospital. Get whatever additional antibiotics they say you need. Follow the doctor's directions to the letter. Get plenty of rest. And, while you're doing all of that, definitely think positive thoughts."

Positive thinking, in my estimation, is the tool you use when every other tool at your disposal has been fully and thoroughly utilized. Otherwise you're asking good thoughts to accomplish something you could just as easily achieve for yourself, by more conventional means. You can hope and pray all you want that you'll win the lottery, but the purchase of lottery tickets will inevitably prove to be a more useful strategy.

So, there you have my thoughts on positive thinking. I'm all for it. I firmly believe the chances are incredibly slim that I will ever again be confronted by two hungry coyotes while walking my dog. It will probably never happen, and if it does, I have no doubt we will come out intact, just the way we did last time. I'm not afraid when I walk, and I don't entertain any bad thoughts.

If there's one thing I'm not, it's a fatalist.

But I still carry the big stick.

The Airport on a Bad Day

Lessons in Empathy

Years ago, I was doing a lot of business travel. And I do mean a lot. I was supplementing my writing income as a public speaker.

It got out of hand, at least by my standards. I was on the road for about a third of the year.

One day I was exhausted and trying to get home when an airline problem caused me to miss a flight out of Phoenix to San Luis Obispo (SLO), my nearest regional airport. And there are only a couple of US Air flights to SLO per day. It's not like American or United out of LAX or SFO, where they go out every couple of hours. The next flight was a seven-hour wait.

I had a bit of a tantrum at the gate, in front of the gate agent. Not pretty, but I was so exhausted and needed so badly to get home.

I stood in the customer service line for an eternity, then vented my frustrations on the customer service agent. I wanted her to find me a flight on another airline to get me home sooner. But there was nothing.

I gave up inside.

"Fine," I said, "I'll just go to the American Airlines lounge."

I wasn't flying AA that day. But this debacle happened to fall into the one year I actually threw for the club membership, because I spent so much time in airports.

I was told the lounge was closed.

Exhausted and discouraged, I rolled my heavy bags to the US Air lounge. Where I did not have a membership.

There I quietly told the woman behind the counter that I would pay the (outrageous—but I don't think I said so out loud) one-time fee if I absolutely had to, but considering how much trouble the airline had caused me that day, I would very much appreciate being comped in.

Here's what she said. And it was a bit of an eye-opener, to say the least.

"Okay, I'll go ahead and do that for you. Because you didn't yell at me. These people come in here, and they yell at me, and I think, 'Why do I want to do anything nice for you? You're yelling at me.'"

I thanked her sincerely, then settled in.

In retrospect, I should have thanked her twice, because she taught me something I've never forgotten.

I sat and looked out the window for several hours. Under the window, baggage handlers drove their carts around in the hot Phoenix sun. I watched them throw bag after bag. And was struck with a very important thought.

Everyone has been working hard. *Everyone* is tired. *Everyone* just wants to go home. My pressing problem was indeed real, and indeed my problem. But it was not in the least unique.

I couldn't find the customer service agent again. But, to my delight, when I got back to the gate, there was the gate agent who had witnessed my tantrum. I apologized sincerely for losing my temper.

He could not have been nicer about it.

Of course, as I mentioned, this all happened years ago. So why did it come up to be written now?

I'm writing this just a couple of days before Christmas. This morning a Twitter friend who works in a mall tweeted that everyone in the world should work one full shift in a mall around the holidays. She said the world would be a better place if they did.

I think she's right.

When I was about seventeen, I waited tables at a Norm's restaurant at Sunset and Vermont in Hollywood. For three whole days. Then the supervisor pulled me aside and told me I wasn't fast enough. And I had to turn in my apron. But three days was enough.

To this very day, almost forty years later, I leave decent tips, and I don't blame the wait staff if the food comes up slowly.

So … I haven't thought too much yet about a New Year's resolution. Staying in the moment always works, and could easily keep me busy, New-Year's-resolution-wise, until the day I die. But now I'm thinking maybe I could resolve to try to see the world through the other person's eyes. Treat them the way I'd want to be treated.

Right, I know. That's nothing but the good old Golden Rule. Not that anything ever needed to be more. I've always said, if we all followed it, the only problems left in the world would be weather related.

So that was a good reminder for myself, and maybe others as well. And what can I say but … here's to good weather in the New Year.

Believe in Yourself

The Path to Publication

Picture *Pay It Forward* in a Drawer

Rejection is inevitable in the life of a writer. And yes, that means I've been rejected. Thousands of times. (Ha, ha, you think. She's exaggerating for effect. No. She's not. Thousands of times.) I used to keep all my short story rejections in a huge box. I thought I'd use them to wallpaper a room someday. I finally threw them away when I realized I would probably never have a room the size of two football fields. I lost count somewhere around 1,500.

Now, you may think only my earlier stories were rejected, and that they met with this fate because they weren't good. Most people don't really understand rejection as it relates to an author. A lot of authors don't really understand rejection as it relates to an author.

Let me clarify:

My average short story was rejected more than seventeen times before going on to find publication … without further revision.

In one case, I received a form rejection with checkboxes for why the story was returned. Boxes were checked for "Story did not hold reader's interest or attention" and "Story was told, not shown." On its next trip out, it was accepted by an editor who stated that stories like mine were his reason for having become an editor in the first place. He went on to nominate it for

Best American Short Stories, the O'Henry Award, and the Pushcart Prize.

In another case a story was rejected thirty times, then won honorable mention in the Raymond Carver Short Story Contest (which I falsely thought would help its chances) then went on to be rejected another twenty-two times, after which it was picked up simultaneously by two magazines at once. I had to disappoint one, and tell them they couldn't have it.

Right. Rejection is not what you think it is. It's very subjective. Even highly popular works have usually been rejected. Most bestsellers were previously rejected.

My novel *Pay It Forward* was rejected. Several times. In fact, it was rejected by *my* agent. The agent I was actually under contract with at the time. This agent shall remain nameless, in the interest of fairness. Because she doesn't come off well in this story at all.

She had agreed to represent me after reading my novel *Walter's Purple Heart*. So I sent her another of my early novels, *Funerals for Horses*. She rejected that one. She said, "I love this. But it doesn't work."

Right, I know. Don't ask me to explain that comment. Ask someone who understands it. If such a person exists.

Around this time, I was approached—solicited, if you will—by another agent. She was much newer. Had a lot less experience. But she had read a short story of mine in a tiny literary journal. And she wrote to me, through the editor of that journal, to ask if I had any work for which I was seeking representation.

Complicated question. I had an agent. A Big Agent. But I also had a novel for which I was seeking representation. *Funerals for Horses.*

I dug out my copy of the agency contract. It stated, quite clearly, that if my agent passed on any of my work, I had a right to go elsewhere with it.

But that's on paper. This was the real world.

I called my Big Agent and asked her if that was going to work in the real world. Despite her being—in my opinion—a trifle professionally jealous, she agreed that it did. Because I had asked. Full disclosure and all that.

I went back to New Agent and asked how she felt about taking on a novel all by itself. That is, without first right of refusal on my future work. Because Big Agent had first right of refusal on all my future work.

She agreed to give it a read.

She loved it enough to take it on all by itself.

For the next and perhaps most interesting (like the ancient Chinese curse "May you live in interesting times") stretch of my journey to publication, I had two agents. I would like to report that I was absolutely correct. It works better on paper than it does in the real world.

There's an old saying in my business that an author's relationship with his or her agent is something like a marriage. Nobody really stops to explain what this means, but I take it to mean that you enter the relationship on a giddy high, just knowing life will be perfect from here on out. And in less than six months you're arguing over who's going to take out the trash.

One woman's opinion.

(I do want to note, however, that I have now had the same agent for eight years, and we could not get along much better. So there is such a thing as a successful marriage.)

If indeed having an agent is something like a marriage, I'd like to report that having two agents is a lot like bigamy. You spend most of your time convincing the one you currently have on the phone that she's the one you really love. And that the other agent means nothing to you.

(You have to believe me! It was one book! It meant nothing!)

If I wanted to make New Agent laugh, I'd tell her, "My other agent doesn't understand me."

Then came the moment of truth. I had just finished my next novel. *Pay It Forward*. I wanted to give it to New Agent. Because she understood me. In fact, I stalled in that work for a long time, and I think that's why. Because I knew when it was done I had to give it to Big Agent. Because Big Agent had the first right of refusal contract.

Now, agency contracts can be cancelled if things just aren't working out. But I was hesitant to cancel this one. Big Agent had owned Big Agency for twenty-five years. A quarter of a century. (Right, you already knew that twenty-five years is a quarter of a century—I just had to stress my point.) She had recently sold world rights to the work of a mutual friend for $100,000. New Agent hadn't yet sold anybody's first fiction.

Hopefully you see the conundrum.

I delivered the *Pay It Forward* manuscript to Big Agent. And patiently waited. Well. Waited.

In time I received a phone message from her. It said, "We need to talk."

We need to talk.

Is that ever good news? *Ever?* Can you just feel your gut turn cold, remembering some of the talks that followed that dreaded statement?

I called her back.

We talked.

She hated it.

I'd like to tell you what she hated about it, but unfortunately I got the impression that it was ... more or less ... everything.

She said, "Why do all the people in it have to be so awful?"

I had just spent quite a bit of time with Reuben and Arlene, and had a hard job framing them in that light. So I said, "You thought Reuben and Arlene were awful?"

"Well," she said. "Maybe awful is the wrong word. But they all had something wrong with them. They all had problems."

Unlike the real world, I was thinking, where we all know nobody ever has any issues.

She said, "Why can't nice people Pay It Forward to other nice people?"

I thought, Right. Good suggestion. I'll write a novel about fictional salvation and people it with characters who don't have any situation in particular from which they need to be saved.

She said, "I don't even know whose story this is."

I said, "I think it's mankind's story."

She snorted and said, "Nobody cares about mankind."

At this point, I more or less stopped listening.

She gave me a great deal more advice on how to take the whole thing apart and put it back together again. But I knew I wouldn't. Because I didn't agree that it was broken.

Late in the conversation (our last one) she got angry and accused me of not listening to her ideas. And that was a fair cop. I'd started out listening. But as our opinions diverged, my listening skills faded.

But the good news was, I had another agent. I could give *Pay It Forward* to New Agent. However, that left the issue of *Walter's Purple Heart*, which had already been rejected some twenty-two times.

"Tell me honestly," I said. "Are you still feeling enthusiastic about *Walter*?"

"Weeeell ... " she said, drawing out the word into several syllables. "It *has* been an awful lot of places."

"Fine," I said. "Send *Walter* home."

We formally terminated our contract. And I gave all my work over to New Agency, which consisted of New Agent and New Agent's Agent Husband.

They sold five books and three movies for me over the next several years. Right up until the time they disbanded the agency to go into a new line of work. One of the books went on to become a national bestseller. It was translated into two-dozen languages. It started an international kindness movement.

And one of the movies actually made it to the big screen.

And the book and the movie were both *Pay It Forward*.

And *Pay It Forward* had not been torn apart and put back together again.

(And, just as a side note, they also sold *Walter's Purple Heart* to the same editor at Simon & Schuster who rejected it when it was with Big Agent. See? Rejection doesn't mean what you think it does.)

Now. What if I had believed Big Agent? What if I hadn't had a second agent to give me a second opinion? What if I hadn't already learned great lessons on the subjectivity of rejection from my endless short story submissions?

That's an easy question to answer. I would have believed her. After all, she was a Big Agent. She'd had Big Agency for twenty-five years. (Did you know that's a quarter of a century?) She sold people's stuff for $100,000. So she knows what will sell and what won't. Right?

Wrong. Nobody does.

If they did, nobody would ever pass on a future best-seller. But agents and editors do, every day. If they knew, they'd never publish highly touted flops. But highly touted flops line the publisher's catalogues every season.

There is no such thing as a book that everyone in the world agrees is a good book. Personally, I despise the work of Ernest Hemingway. If I'd been his contemporary, I'd have been the first to tell Papa not to quit his day job. Imagine Hemingway giving up his writing career just because *I* don't like what he does.

Imagine the manuscript of *Pay It Forward* sitting in a drawer because my ex-agent didn't find it to her liking.

There's always going to be someone who doesn't like what you do. There will always be a few who think you're a genius and others who think you're a hack. That doesn't really matter. It matters what you think. It matters that you believe in yourself at least enough to get a second opinion.

Speaking of believing in yourself, it was eight long, scary years from the time I quit my day job to the time I made a profit from my writing. I worked tiny part-time jobs that didn't get in my way. I sank deeply into debt. Well, maybe not too deeply. Depends on how you look at it. From the point of view of the money I had to live on at the time, it was massive. From the point of view of my life right after this story, it was nothing to sweat about. But before the story was over, I sweated. A lot. I'd wake up in the middle of the night sweating. Thinking how much money I owed, and how little money I had.

Here's how I'd get myself back to sleep. I'd ask myself, "Do you believe in yourself? Because if you don't, you never should have gotten yourself in so deep to begin with. And if you do, it doesn't matter."

Each time, I chose to believe in myself, and go back to sleep.

The publication of *Pay It Forward* put me right back in the black. So it didn't matter.

And that rejection from my agent didn't matter. None of them do. Unless you decide that's the final submission. Until then, the story can always have a happy ending. The unhappy ending comes only when you give up and go home.

Let Life Itself Inspire and Direct and Help and Change You

Moving Off Pressure

How To Find a Good Dog

It's heart-rending to lose a good dog. And I can't help noticing that a lot of people react to it by swearing off dogs forever. They don't want to set themselves up for that kind of pain, ever again. And they just know that no new dog can ever replace the one they lost.

That last part is indeed true. The new dog won't be the same as the old dog. The new spouse is not the same as the old spouse, either. But most people try to love again.

Most. Not all.

Now me, I need a dog in my life. I can't imagine living without one for long. It leaves this big space in my life, a hole the size and shape of a good dog. It's just too hard to work around that emptiness.

My amazing Jenny died in 1991. To give you some idea of the type of dog she was, my sister used to ask, "I wonder who's really inside that little black dog suit?" She wasn't really so little. About forty-five pounds. I rescued her when she was five. And she only lived to be ten.

May I officially say, No fair?

Well, sure I can. And may. But she'll still be gone.

I only waited about two weeks. It was just too hard to go to bed at night. I had always called her when it was time to go to bed, and we'd go in together. I was staying up too late. Losing too much sleep. I had to try to fill that great dog-shaped hole.

Now, I didn't publish my first novel until 1997. But I've been a full-time writer since 1991. In other words, I was very poor at this juncture of my life.

I drove to the county pound. Walked in the front door. And was confronted by a sign that informed me that dog adoptions cost sixty-six dollars. In fairness, most of that is a spay or neuter deposit, and covers their shots, and lots of other things I'd need to pay for anyway, even if I got a dog for free.

All of which failed to change the simple fact that I did not have sixty-six dollars in my pocket.

I drove home in defeat.

It was a couple of days before my birthday. I wanted to give myself a new dog for my birthday. But it was more than I could afford at that moment.

The following day I received a birthday card from my father. With a fifty-dollar bill tucked inside.

The day after that (April sixteenth, the day before my birthday) I added my own sixteen dollars to it, drove back to the county pound, and met Jessie for the first time.

She had been surrendered by her owner the night before. In other words, she had not been there yet the last time I showed up.

She was in such bad shape that they were only going to give her two days. I guess they figured no fool would adopt a dog who looked so bad.

They hadn't met this fool yet.

It was hard to believe a dog in such bad condition hadn't been picked up on the street.

She had mange, and every square inch of her body had just a handful of hairs on it. Her skin was flaking into dandruff.

She had patches of thick, roughened "elephant skin" where she'd been biting.

One long strand of hair hanging from her tail, literally just one, signaled that she'd once had a long coat.

She weighed about thirty-five pounds. Her proper weight was between forty-five and fifty. You could see every knob of her backbone. From across the room.

Her head was down, her tail between her legs. She was too easily intimidated to be in a cage with two other big dogs.

In that lighting, I couldn't see her coat and skin very clearly. I could tell she was scruffy and in bad shape, but I didn't quite see how bad.

But I did see one thing about her I really liked. She looked up at me. And she had one blue eye. One blue, one brown. I've always been fascinated by that in a dog.

I asked the kennel guy to take her out. He kept thinking he misunderstood me.

"That one?" he said. Like there must be some kind of mistake.

"Yes. That one." What part of "that one" don't you understand, I refrained from saying.

But the question had an obvious answer. He simply could not understand why anyone would pick that one.

She put her paws up on my shoulders and snuffled my face. When I touched her, I was touching mostly bare skin. That's when I realized she probably had mange, not just overall scruffiness. My heart sank. My mom had a dog at home, a black lab. How could I bring mange into the house? I'd be putting her at risk. I told the kennel guy, "You'd better put her back."

As I watched him lead her into the cage, I knew that would probably be the second last walk she'd ever take.

I drove to Woods Humane, and looked at their dogs. They had a batch of lovely little Aussie puppies with blue eyes. I held one. I remember saying to him, out loud, "I'm putting you back now, but don't worry. You'll get a home. Everybody wants you. I'm going back and getting that one nobody wants."

I called the vet to be sure he could fit her in. Right then. Before I even brought her home. And we kept her apart from my mom's dog until we were sure her mange was totally cured.

My friends mostly thought I was insane. One said Jessie looked like a victim of radiation poisoning. Another accused me of having a Florence Nightingale complex.

My friend Pat was the most kind. She took one look at Jessie and said, "No, she's beautiful. She's a real Charlie Brown's Christmas tree of a dog."

She gained weight fast. Grew a healthy, long, beautiful coat in black and silver. Against odds, she turned into a lovely dog. Her before and after photos were nothing short of astonishing.

Jessie was a year and a half old when I adopted her, and she lived until May of 2006. She was closer to seventeen than to sixteen when she died, and in perfect health for all but the last month or so. She was gentle and sweet almost to a fault, wooed cats into being her friends, cared for my mom's new puppy when she arrived, and, most amazing of all, learned to be happy.

And she helped me learn to be happy, too.

My Charlie Brown's Christmas tree of a dog decorated beautifully.

I'd had only a two-day window in which to find her. And I had been about to miss it. But circumstances beyond my control slowed me down just enough. Got me there at just the right time.

I sure wouldn't have wanted to miss Jessie.

When she died, I could no longer use that old excuse, "But she won't be Jessie. She won't be the same as the dog I lost." Because I was mourning the death of a great dog when I met Jessie. She didn't replace Jenny. She wasn't Jenny. But the fact that she was Jessie turned out to be plenty good enough.

I made another trip to the county pound. And, for the first time in my life, I picked out the wrong dog.

He was this goofy-looking eight-month-old black lab. Big, maybe sixty pounds. A boy. Just as sweet as he could be. The pound people told me he had only been there for a couple of days. So they couldn't tell me much about him. Well, what do you need to know about a black lab puppy? They're sweet.

I named him Mateo (which nobody seemed to like, and I couldn't imagine why not) and took him home.

Within a matter of hours, he was attacking my mom's little twenty-pound, fifteen-year-old terrier mix. Just for walking through the room. He was also beginning to have a strange and threatening reaction to anyone who tried to approach me. A nervous shifting of his body. A weird series of noises in his throat.

I had to do something I've never done before in my life. I had to take a dog back to the pound. And I wasn't happy about it. In fact, the next morning, as I waited with him for the pound to open its doors, I was in tears.

I expected people to be kind about it. I mean, I gave it my best. It just didn't work out. I can't adopt a dog who wants to kill the dog who already lives there. It's a deal-breaker. It's an untenable situation.

Except in the eyes of the woman I spoke to that morning at the pound.

She treated me like I was the enemy. Like I was every irresponsible loser who ever abandoned a dog for no compelling reason. I didn't want to be treated like an irresponsible dog owner. I felt I was a very responsible dog person, and that, as such, my first responsibility was to the dog I already had.

When I tried to explain the seriousness of what he had done, she dismissed me with a simple, "All dogs do that. That's just what dogs do."

Now, I used to train dogs for a living. For years. And while I concede that competition among dogs is nothing new, I will stand by my assessment that most big male black lab puppies will not go after a much smaller, much older female. And not every dog feels the need to be top dog.

I didn't get to share any of those thoughts with her. She announced, rather harshly, that she had to get to work. And she left, leading Mateo after her.

I could not have felt worse. I literally cannot remember being in more of a funk. I got in my car and drove back to the highway. I started to get into the left lane to turn toward home. But I didn't want to go home feeling so bad. I wanted to do something, anything, to help my mood.

I made an impulsive right. Turned south. I had decided suddenly that I would go over the county line into Santa Maria and check the dogs at their pound. Maybe I would find the one I was really meant to have. There was just one problem. I didn't know where the county pound was located in Santa Maria. But I had my cell phone with me. So I called.

Now, here's where it gets interesting. In my mind, anyway. And here's where it plays into my theme, my point, which I swear I'm getting to. As always, thank you for your patience.

It was after nine. The Santa Maria Pound should, by all rights, have been open. Somebody should have answered the phone. Instead I got a recorded message. It said the pound was located on West Blosser Road.

I knew where Blosser Road was. I could find my way to that. Except, when I got down there, there *was* no West Blosser Road. There was only a North and South Blosser.

I drove around for a while, then called the pound again. This time someone picked up.

"Where are you?" I asked. "I'm having more trouble finding you. There *is* no West Blosser Road."

A brief silence. "You're on Blosser Road?"

"Yeah. Where are you?"

"We're on West *Foster* Road."

Foster. Oh. Damn. Really sounded like Blosser on the recorded message. Or maybe I wasn't getting the best reception.

"So … " I ventured, " … how far away are you?"

"All the way on the other side of town," he said.

I breathed deeply, then told him never mind all that, it didn't matter. If he could just direct me, I'd drive across town and find the place.

He didn't direct me.

Instead he asked, "Are you looking for a dog?"

I'm still not sure why he asked that. I could have been surrendering an animal. I could have been looking for a cat. Did I need a dog so badly that he could hear it in my voice?

"Because if you're looking for a dog, you're right around the corner from the Santa Maria Valley Humane Society."

I had never heard of it. I had not known it existed.

He directed me there instead.

And there I met Ella.

She was only four months old. She didn't even tip the scales in double digits. (The first week I had her, I took her with me to the mailing center to meet their two sweet golden retrievers, and the owner put her on the postal scale. Nine pounds.) Each of her ears was about as big as the whole rest of her head. They stuck straight up. She had square, knobby knees that seemed to sit almost right on top of her paws.

She was happy to meet me, to put it mildly.

She just happened to be in a place I never knew existed. So how was I going to find her there? It took a little doing on the part of the Universe. It took a couple of redirecting pushes.

Now for the part about moving off pressure. Maybe you've been curious about that the whole time you've been reading this. Or maybe you've forgotten it entirely. If so, I don't blame you. I'm coming at this one the long way around.

Remember I told you earlier I used to have a horse? Cody? And that I gentled him myself?

There's a lot you have to teach a horse. And not all of it involves allowing you on his back. You have to teach them ground manners.

They have to be halter-broke, of course, and they need to learn to lead and tie calmly. When you run your hand down the back of their leg, toward the hoof, and give the pastern a little squeeze, they're supposed to shift their weight to the other side and lift that hoof for you. Horses are massive animals. You can't be strong-arming them around. You can't allow them to lean on you while you pick stones out of the frog of their hoof. You don't want to be physically wrenching their hoof up off the ground.

You need a little cooperation.

One of the things I taught my horse was to move off pressure. If I wanted him to take a step over with his front legs, I pushed gently on his shoulder. If I wanted him to take a step over with his back legs, I pushed gently on his flank.

He learned that my goal was to get him to move away from that pressure. It's a gentle signal. It involves no force or violence. It's a quiet language for how I mean to position him.

Take it even a step further and you have neck-reining, in which you never pull on the bit in the horse's mouth to steer him. Instead you move the reins to the right, and when he feels the gentle pressure of the reins on his neck, he steers right.

There are much more violent ways to handle a horse. But why use violence when the gentle ways work fine?

My point here is that, in my honest opinion, the Universe steers me. You can agree with this or disagree. But if you pay attention to this in your own life, you might be surprised.

Here's the advantage of paying attention: I think the Universe aims to steer me gently. If possible. If that seems to be working. But when all else fails, there's always the old mule-training trick. They say, "First you hit the mule between the eyes with a two-by-four. That's to get his attention."

Ever heard that one?

If so, you probably get my point about why it's best to pay attention.

So here's my theory on how to find a good dog. Or, for that matter, how to find a good anything.

Try to move off pressure.

If you think you know which way you want to go, but doors keep slamming in your face, look around and see if another door is open.

Rather than being furious that your best plan didn't work out, maybe be open to the idea that the plan might not have been as good as you thought.

Go where you feel yourself being steered.

As a final note, if you're thinking poor Mateo was the big loser in this story, I want to add that his tale (tail?) appears to have had a happy ending as well. A friend in the local writing community once told me his wife was a volunteer at the pound. So I called her, and we talked about my experiences with the dog. At length. Because they need to know this stuff, to get dogs into the right homes.

Later she told me that a family with kids came in, and wanted to adopt him. They were discouraged from doing so, based on the information I'd provided. Then a couple came in and wanted him. They were filled in on his situation. But they said that was no problem. They had no kids, no other dogs, and they wanted him to be protective.

So, by adopting him, and taking him home for the night, I not only got to the right dog for me, I helped get him to the right home for him.

Sometimes I wonder if anything that happens to us is ever a mistake.

The Zen masters say, "There is absolutely nothing wrong with this moment."

As I was heading down the freeway into Santa Maria, crying, I might have argued with that assessment.

Now I think it sounds about right.

Be Grateful for the Good Things You Already Have

Thanksgiving

Gratitude of the Daily and Yearly Variety

I don't save gratitude for any one time of the year.

I love Thanksgiving. Always have, since I was a kid. (Well … I remember having yearly tantrums when forced to wear a dress to dinner, but that's another story for another essay.)

I liked it because I felt it was right—no, more than right, essential—to focus on what we have. It's human nature to take all we're given and focus on what we still want, but it's not the best of human nature. It's a tendency worth counteracting.

Because of that, I find something to be grateful for every day. Usually in the morning. And I post it on Twitter, Facebook, Google+, MySpace and LinkedIn. I use the hashtag #DailyGratitude. (The # is a Twitter tag that helps identify it as a meme. Confused? Yeah, me too. But that's how you do it on Twitter, so the posts show up in a search feed.)

Now, the part about posting gratitude on social networks might sound odd. It might even sound like an idea that doesn't mesh with the gratitude theme. I can picture you asking yourself (I'm a novelist, I have a vivid imagination), *Why online? Why not just be grateful?*

I tried that. It worked fine.

Until I forgot.

Which I always did.

But then I started to be publicly grateful. And within a few days, people were telling me that they liked my #DailyGratitudes. That they followed them. Looked forward to them. Not scads of people, just a handful. Just enough to create accountability. If I slacked off, someone would notice.

I thought I'd been doing this since the beginning of the year, but I just reread my Daily Gratitude posts, all the way back to when I started doing them, on my Facebook timeline. It was clear that I had been doing the #DailyGratitude thing for longer than I thought. Since a year ago October, as of this writing.

I mention this because I want you to know that the #DailyGratitude posts I'm about to use as examples were not made up for the sake of this essay. They are straight off my Facebook timeline. Real posts from real days.

I set out to focus on a specific type of gratitude. Not because I already knew what was most important, but because I didn't want to seem braggy.

I might think, *I'm glad I own my home instead of renting*, or, *I'm glad I'm published as an author*, but I would never use those for my #DailyGratitude. Because I didn't want people to react by thinking, *Sure, I'd be grateful too if I had that.* (Not that I have a lot. Just that I have a lot compared to some. Almost everybody has a lot compared to some.)

Instead I looked for the kind of gratitude that almost anyone can find. The kind that just involves shifting my focus—looking and listening in a different way.

For example …

I still remember the first time I lay awake in bed and listened to the birds singing at dawn. I honestly didn't know if it was something unusual, or if they did that every morning and I just hadn't thought to listen.

And I never used to look up much when I was outside, until one day I noticed how the clouds looked as though they'd been painted on. I felt as if I could see the brush strokes. So I started commenting about the Painter of the Clouds. And now I notice the clouds all the time. And they are so often amazing!

Everybody's grateful for a beautiful spring or summer day. So in spring I'd share things like:

> This little dwarf rosebush—a volunteer. Came right up through a crack in the pavement of my yard. #DailyGratitude

And:

> Looked out the window, saw drops of fog mist on pine needles. Decided to devote my #DailyGratitude to the sight.

And:

> A gazillion California poppies on The Ranch. Yes, a gazillion exactly. I counted. #DailyGratitude

And then in summer:

When the moon is full, and I look out my back window in the dark, the white calla lilies seem to glow. #DailyGratitude

And:

Peaches. I am grateful for peaches. Maybe that's why they don't grow year 'round. So we can be more grateful for them. #DailyGratitude

And then it rolled around to autumn, but that turned out to be equally easy, at least for me. So I'd post things like:

26 years on the coast, and I still gasp with joy when I see a chevron of 30+ brown pelicans glide between me and the sun. #DailyGratitude

And:

Surf is crashing, Farmer's Market has turned to pumpkins and pomegranates. I trust the seasons and all other forms of change. #DailyGratitude

And:

Kayaking, the birds leave their beautiful feathers as presents for me on the surface of the water. I pick them up with my paddle. #DailyGratitude

But winter is supposed to be harder, I guess. (Only maybe not in Cambria.) Still, I was in the swing of things by then, and had no trouble at all:

236 yards from the ocean, when the surf is high and rough, like it is now, I can lie in bed and listen to it crash. #DailyGratitude

And:

Don't like the wind, but like to watch birds flying in it. Some hang still. Watched a crow flap its wings and fly backward. #DailyGratitude

And:

My little dog Ella joins me for "Yoga by the fire" on Winter mornings. She basks, I do Yoga. Well ... she does a good down dog. #DailyGratitude

And:

38 degrees outside and a perfect fire in the wood stove, crackling as I write this. #DailyGratitude

But what about the days that are really hard? What about just flat-out lousy days? I have my share. Don't we all? But I managed to come up with something anyway. Usually something pretty honest. Something that didn't try to mask the fact that I was having a bad day. Like:

> Grateful that, when I can't sleep at night, Ella's tucked up close. And warm. #DailyGratitude

Or:

> Sometimes I feel a bit lonely, but I know everybody is out there. I just forget to reach. Thanks for being out there. #DailyGratitude

Or:

> When someone is unkind, it reminds me how much kindness I encounter every day. And it reminds me to be kinder. #DailyGratitude

Or:

> Today I am able to breathe deeply and know that all is/will be okay. It always was before. #DailyGratitude

With practice, it kept getting easier.

On mornings when I had something going on, like an early paddle in my kayak, I'd post something like:

> Early morning kayak. Only birds were up. Brought my camera & camcorder in a dry bag. Videoed an otter doing the backstroke. #DailyGratitude

On morning with nothing at all going on, it would be something more like:

> On unscheduled mornings, I like to lie awake in bed and hear how the birds greet the day. They never seem jaded about it. #DailyGratitude

When I was going away on a great trip, I'd post:

> I am deeply grateful for our national parks. They give us a place to go to recreate ourselves. I will stand to protect them. #DailyGratitude

And when I got home:

> My own bed. With the flannel sheets. In my own house. With my own Ella pup under the covers with me. Nice to be home. #DailyGratitude

On rainy days, I'd post:

It's a beautiful rainy day/week. Thanks for giving our still-somewhat-thirsty state a drink of water. #DailyGratitude

And on sunny ones:

The Painter of the Clouds is taking a well-earned day off. And Ella and I are taking a 7-mile walk under blue skies. #DailyGratitude

When I hiked, I'd post:

My #DailyGratitude is late because I was out living it. Ella and I hiked a very steep trail in Big Sur, very early. #GrandCanyon-hereIcome

And when I didn't:

Yesterday I was grateful for 21 miles hiked. Today I'm grateful to just sit in my comfy chair. #DailyGratitude

And then there were those Daily Gratitude posts for the things you just can't classify. Like:

That lovely moment when it's suddenly possible to grasp that we are exactly where we are meant to be. #DailyGratitude

And:

I am getting better—not perfect, but no-
ticeably better—at letting the little t
hings go. #DailyGratitude

And:

Everything that happens to me in life,
whether I like it or not, seems to steer me
down the right path. #DailyGratitude

And:

Got up early to hear a speaker from Rwan-
da who lost both hands in the genocide.
Why aren't I more grateful for my hands?
#DailyGratitude

And:

I dreamed my dog was lost, but she was
under the covers with me the whole time.
Sometimes we are more okay than we
know. #DailyGratitude

Here's what I learned from my Daily Gratitude:
the blessings I decided to focus on just coincidentally
happen to be the ones that really matter. In the great
scheme of life, it's not about whether I own or rent,
whether I'm published or not published. What matters
is the way the birds sing at dawn, and the amazing
way the clouds are painted on the sky.

But I had to be grateful first. And then my gratitude led me to a better understanding of what to be grateful for. Funny how that works.

And the Path Continues

mean … we want it to. Don't we? Because we don't stop walking this long, steep path until the day the folks we've left behind lay us to rest. When that day comes, I'll accept what is. But I'm sure in no hurry.

Every day brings something more to ask of myself, or to stop asking of myself. Chances to be with people and to be alone. Moments to stay in, good and bad to accept. More #DailyGratitude thoughts to post.

It's not often easy and it's not always fun. But it seems to be what we have. So I greet it with the best cheer I can muster.

And that, as best one can describe such an elusive phenomenon, is how I continue to find the life I want in the life I already have. When you think about it, where else would you find it?

Author's Note

Every story in this book is drawn from my own experience. A small minority of these stories involve actual people I have known. Of the seven or so essays that do, only one of the persons I describe is living. In that case, I sent the story to her in advance to be sure she was comfortable with my using it in this book.

Some of the people described in these pages were members of the program of Alcoholics Anonymous, and in those cases I refer to them by first name only. In extremely limited instances (really just, "Slowly, slowly," and, "… but, it's okay …") I related something said in the context of a meeting. That said, I exercised extreme care to assure that I did not violate the anonymity of any AA member.

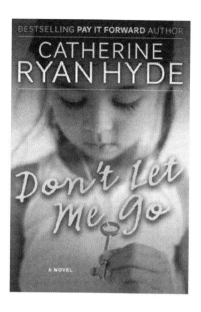

"An excellent read."
–New Books Review

"Original and wonderful."
–The Sun

"Catherine Ryan Hyde at her utter best."
–ChickLit Reviews

The U.K. bestseller is now available in the U.S. for the first time!

Former Broadway dancer and current agoraphobic Billy Shine has not set foot outside his apartment in almost a decade. He has glimpsed his neighbors—beautiful manicurist Rayleen, lonely old Ms. Hinman, bigoted and angry Mr. Lafferty, kind-hearted Felipe, and 9-year-old Grace and her former addict mother Eileen.

But most of them have never seen Billy. Not until Grace begins to sit outside on the building's front stoop for hours every day, inches from Billy's patio. Troubled by this change in the natural order, Billy makes it far enough out onto his porch to ask Grace why she doesn't sit inside where it's safe. Her answer: "If I sit inside, then nobody will know I'm in trouble. And then nobody will help me."

Her answer changes everything.

By the bestselling author of WHEN I FOUND YOU, SECOND HAND HEART, and PAY IT FORWARD, DON'T LET ME GO is the heart-breaking, funny, and life-affirming story of a building full of loners and misfits who come together to help a little girl survive—and thrive—against all odds.

BUY YOUR COPY TODAY!

About Catherine Ryan Hyde

Catherine Ryan Hyde is the author of 20 published and forthcoming books. Her newer novels include *When I Found You, Second Hand Heart, Don't Let Me Go,* and *When You Were Older.* New Kindle editions of her earlier titles *Funerals for Horses, Earthquake Weather and Other Stories, Electric God,* and *Walter's Purple Heart* are now available. Her newest ebook title is *The Long Steep Path: Everyday Inspiration from the Author of PAY IT FORWARD,* her first book-length creative nonfiction. Forthcoming frontlist titles are *Walk Me Home* and *Where We Belong.*

She is co-author, with publishing industry blogger Anne R. Allen, of *How to Be a Writer in the E-Age… and Keep Your E-Sanity!*

Her best-known novel, *Pay It Forward,* was adapted into a major motion picture, chosen by the American Library Association for its Best Books for Young Adults list, and translated into more than 23 languages for distribution in over 30 countries. The paperback was released in October 2000 by Pocket Books and quickly became a national bestseller. *Love in the Present Tense* enjoyed bestseller status in the UK, where it broke the top ten, spent five weeks on the national bestseller list, was reviewed on a major TV book club, and shortlisted for a Best Read of the Year award at the British Book Awards. Both *Becoming Chloe* and *Jumpstart the World* were included on the ALA's Rainbow List, and *Jumpstart the World* was a finalist for two Lambda Literary Awards.

More than 50 of her short stories have been published in The Antioch Review, Michigan Quarterly Review, The Virginia Quarterly Review, Ploughshares, Glimmer Train and many other journals, and in the anthologies Santa Barbara Stories and California Shorts and the bestselling anthology Dog is my Co-Pilot. Her stories have been honored in the Raymond Carver Short Story Contest and the Tobias Wolff Award and nominated for Best American Short Stories, the O'Henry Award, and the Pushcart Prize. Three have been cited in Best American Short Stories.

Catherine is founder and former president (2000-2009) of the Pay It Forward Foundation. As a professional public speaker she has addressed the National Conference on Education, twice spoken at Cornell University, met with Americorps members at the White House and shared a dais with Bill Clinton.

For more information, please visit the author at catherineryanhyde.com.

Also by Catherine Ryan Hyde

Fiction

Walk Me Home

When You Were Older

Don't Let Me Go

Second Hand Heart

When I Found You

Electric God/The Hardest Part of Love

Funerals for Horses

Walter's Purple Heart

Earthquake Weather and Other Stories

Jumpstart the World

Diary of a Witness

The Day I Killed James

Chasing Windmills

The Year of My Miraculous Reappearance

Love in the Present Tense

Becoming Chloe
Pay It Forward

Non-fiction

How to be a Writer in the E-Age...And Keep Your
E-Sanity

Made in the USA
Middletown, DE
03 December 2016